THE PHOTOCOPIABLE
ROMAN
BRITAIN
ACTIVITY BOOK

Written by Paul Cross
Illustrated by John Hutchinson

A Photocopiable Teacher Resource Book for Primary Classes

Studying Roman Britain

Published by
TOPICAL RESOURCES

ROMAN
BRITAIN

by _____

Class _____

Introduction

A 'Topic' is an approach to teaching in a Primary School which involves various apparently unrelated tasks being carried out under the umbrella of a common title or theme such as 'Roman Britain'.

Topic work always:

- includes class, group and individual work with some element of choice.
- involves practical activities.
- uses themes selected which are thought appropriate to the interests and stage of development of the children involved.
- involves first hand experiences such as a visit or visitors.
- involves some sort of investigation.
- involves information gathering skills.
- crosses some curriculum boundaries.

    It should also include, if possible, an element of *FUN.*

The purpose of this book is to provide a bank of ideas and photocopiable activities, based on the study of Roman Britain, which fulfil the above criteria. It is envisaged that a busy class teacher will use his or her professional judgement to select activities appropriate to their own individual situation.

Copyright © 1999 Paul Cross

Illustrated by John Hutchinson

Printed in Great Britain for **Topical Resources**
Publishers of Educational Materials,
P.O. Box 329
Broughton,
Preston
PR3 5LT

Telephone (01772) 863158

by T. Snape & Company Limited
Bolton's Court,
Preston

PR1 3TY

Typeset by 'ArtWorks' (01772) 431010

Published January 1999

ISBN: 1-872977-40-5

Contents

Background Information for Class Lessons

The Celts

Any study of Roman Britain should start with a view of the society that existed in Britain before the Roman occupation of the island. Britain was populated by many Celtic tribes, who had been developing their own ways and society in the island for about fifteen hundred years before the Roman's arrival in Britain.

Celtic Tribal Organisation

There were approximately thirty Celtic tribes in the mainland of Britain ruled over by tribal kings, who frequently fought over land with neighbouring tribes in long running tribal feuds. The tribal rulers had established large fortified village headquarters in hill forts, often with complex earthworks. A fine example of these earthworks still exists at Maiden Castle, Dorset.

The tribes were ruled through an oligarchy of noble families, with lower families and slaves (captives from tribal wars) providing the workers. Celtic society was agricultural with arable and animal farming forming the food sources. Tribal wars were fought by a very mobile mounted cavalry and charioteers who had spear throwers on their chariots. Warriors would hone up their fighting techniques training their young nobles in the art of warfare. They would be painted with intricate patterned body tattoos and use blue woad face paint. Battles were fierce and blood thirsty with the victors decapitating their foes and storing the heads in jars believing that they had caught the bravery and strength of their enemies to add to their own. The tribal warfare often led to alliances of tribes fighting to overcome each other. Some southern tribes had begun to form alliances with Celtic tribes in northern Gaul (France) to fight the Roman invasion of Gaul.

Celtic Crafts

Within the tribes metal working craft in first iron and then bronze was very active providing weapons for war and agricultural tools. At first these crafts were carried out alongside agricultural duties, but by the century before the Roman invasion of the island there had developed within most tribes skilled metal-workers who were providing their tribes with weapons but more importantly a huge artistic range of personal jewellery. Much of this jewellery displays the intricate curved and inter-locking designs typical of Celtic art. This metal industry had begun to trade its goods beyond the shores of the island. To service this growing craft industry many mines and metal smelting centres had grown up. The change in organisation of craftsmen may have been responsible for the growth of tribal centres away from the hilltops and into valley sites which have been seen by some archaeologists as the precursors of the later Roman towns.

Celtic Religious Practices

The Celts worship was basically naturalistic with their most sacred places being woods, springs, rivers and lakes. Their religious leaders played a very important part in everyday Celtic life and as such were revered and given a place in the tribal hierarchy only just below that of the ruling family. They have come to be known by the name the Romans gave them, 'Druids.' No major tribal decision would be made without consulting the God who was that tribe's oracle. An acknowledgement of these priests' role in the life of the Celtic tribes of Britain comes with the importance the early Roman occupiers placed on expelling them from the island.

Julius Caesar's Invasion Attempt

The desire for military glory which could be displayed in Rome had led Julius Caesar to campaign and occupy large areas of Gaul. By this conquest he sought to preserve his position and reputation. His campaigns in Gaul had been frustrated or made more difficult because of the involvement of Celtic tribes by alliance with their Celtic neighbours in Gaul. These are some causes for Julius Caesar's two expeditions to Britain in 55 and 54 B.C., though no one knows his real reasons for these visits or whether he intended a permanent conquest of the island. Caesar's close shaves against the Celts of Britain in battle and against the elements provided practical lessons for future invasions and set important precedents for the future Roman intervention in Britain.

Julius Caesar had received the surrender of tribal kings in south eastern Britain. He had accepted the friendship of other leaders, and an annual tax to Rome had been imposed on the British Celts. Julius Caesar had installed as king of the Tinovantes tribe of Essex a young prince who had fled to him in Gaul. The father of this prince had been killed in battle by Cassivellaunus the Celtic tribal chief who had lead an alliance of British tribes against Caesar's expedition. Caesar's military victories had enabled him to demand that Cassivellaunus's alliance leave the Trinovantes tribe in peace. Rome could then after Julius Caesar's expedition claim lordship of an area of Britain and the right to extract payments along with an obligation to protect those tribes who had supported the Roman intervention in the island's tribal squabbles.

The Claudian Invasion of Britain

For almost a century Rome drew some tribute from

Background Information for Class Lessons

Britain and continued alliances with friendly tribes in the island. When Claudius was unexpectedly thrust onto the imperial throne of Rome following the assassination of Caligula, he felt the need to appease the army leaders, who had brought him into power, with some military conquest and glory. The fact that there were two Celtic princes from Britain begging for Roman help to put them in power in a Celtic tribal dispute in the island gave Claudius an excuse for an invasion of the distant island across the 'ocean' as the Romans referred to the English Channel.

So in A.D. 43 Claudius ordered the invasion of Britain.The force, which was assembled to sail to Britain, comprised of four legions and as many auxiliary troops numbering 40,000 men. Against the discipline, organisation and fighting prowess of this Roman force the British tribes could only summon their aristocratic charioteers and the levies of farm labourers and slaves. In ambush and surprise attack the Celts could harm the might of Roman military force, but the Roman Generals built well stocked fortified camps, and chose open battle grounds where their infantry and javelin throwers could overcome the Celts. Then the hill fort strong holds of the tribes were overcome by the Roman siege weaponry.

Perhaps the greatest factor in the Roman army's success was the fact that it could stay in the field all year round owing to its professional nature and supply organisation. The Celts on the other hand could only rely on a part time army of farmers who were tied to return at different times of the year to work their farms. Thus it was that Claudius was able to crown his fifteen day visit to the island with a triumphal entry into Colchester, accompanied by elephants, to receive the homage of eleven Celtic tribal chiefs. By 47 A.D. the Roman army commanded Britain as far as the Rivers Severn and Trent.

Boudicca's Revolt

The Romans governed Britain following the conquest of the southern part of England after 47 A.D. through a succession of military Governors. They came to rely on 'client' kings of friendly tribes to control the country. The island had a large force of many legions, which were the guarantee of peace for the regions the Romans had conquered. For a period there was peace, the taxes were paid to Rome. The economy of the Roman empire benefited greatly from the state run silver mines of the Mendip Hills. All seemed well as long as the Romans did not venture northwards or westwards to clash with the warring tribes of the North of England and Wales. In A.D. 61 Prasutagus King of the Icenii tribe of East Anglia died leaving half of his possessions to the Roman Emperor, expecting in return protection for his family and tribe from the Romans. Agents of the Roman governor treated the dead King's bequest as total surrender to Rome. They confiscated the King's property, nobles of the tribe were expelled from their estates, harsh taxes were imposed and conscription of the young warriors of the tribe into the Roman auxiliary forces was enforced.

When the king's widow Boudicca protested she was flogged and her daughters were raped. Rousing her tribe and other discontented local tribes Boudicca swept through southern England, burning Colchester, London and St. Albans. Romans and Roman sympathisers were tortured and murdered. Roman units left in the area were defeated. Paulinus, the Roman general and governor of the province heard of the revolt as he was suppressing the Druid cult in its power base in Anglesey. His legions marched to the Midlands of England and massacred the rebel tribes in battle.

Boudicca fled the battle and poisoned herself in a sacred oak grove to join the eighty thousand warriors who had fallen to the disciplined fighting of the Roman legions. Roman Rule extended to the whole island. In the 60 years following the revolt of the tribes a different policy of Romanisation of Britain was pursued. Tribal kings and their nobles were pensioned off to live in Roman villas on their lands. Young nobles and their tribal warriors were encouraged to join the Roman legions with the bait of becoming full Roman citizens on their retirement.

No longer did Rome attempt to rule through client tribal leaders, the power of the Celtic tribes was reduced. Towns were more heavily fortified, retiring Roman legionaries from all over the Empire were given farms surrounding these towns The whole colony was ruled by Roman governors in charge of areas of the country. A greater effort was made to make the towns more Roman. Trade was encouraged, public baths and water supplies, theatres, temples amphitheatres, town villas and forums were built. In this way the towns came to rule the surrounding countryside where the majority of the native Celts still lived.

A series of brilliant generals overcame the warlike tribes of the North and Wales. Roman rule was extended as far as the Highlands of Scotland after fierce battles with the local tribes.

The Initiatives of Hadrian

A man of restless energy and vitality the Emperor

Background Information for Class Lessons

Hadrian made it his policy to tour the provinces of the Empire. One of the few emperors to set himself against further expansion of the Empire, he was unpopular with the noble ruling families of Rome. He pursued many novel initiatives throughout the Roman Empire. In Britain there were three major initiatives. Started in 128 A.D. Hadrian's Wall was built on a line that the Romans had withdrawn to because of the resistance of the tribes in Scotland to earlier Roman expansion. The idea of a linked defensive line, well supplied with effective communication roads, was brilliant. Its construction far exceeded the original plans and estimates as to its cost.

Hadrian's second initiative in Britain was to colonise the Fenland of East Anglia. This involved huge water engineering projects, unfortunately the farms for veterans established on reclaimed land survived no more than fifty years. Hadrian's rebuilding and expansion of Londinium (London) as provincial capital was more lasting. The former forum and basilica were demolished, a new forum and extensive new public buildings were erected and the whole city site extended to twice its former size. By 46 A.D. Rome had consolidated its command and control of its British province.

Religion in Roman Britain

The most telling evidence for the integration of Celtic and Roman ways of life comes in the area of religious worship. Roman Britain was a religious kaleidoscope, with remains of different sites dedicated to Roman, Greek, Eastern European, Belgian, Hispanic and Celtic gods being found throughout Britain. This breadth of religious practice perhaps only mirrors the diversity of the Roman troops with recruits from all over the vast Roman empire serving in Britain and raising monuments to their Gods during their service in the island. However, through all this diversity some definite pattern can be discerned. There emerges from archaeological evidence an amalgamation of worship of classical Roman and Celtic gods. So from Weardale comes an altar stone to Silvanus (a Celtic God of the woods) raised by a Roman cavalry officer in thanks for successful hunting. At Bath the Roman goddess of wisdom, Minerva, is linked with the local Celtic god of healing springs, Sulis.

On Hayling Island a Celtic shrine is rebuilt and rededicated to joint Romano-Celtic gods. Both cultures have at the base of their religious practice a belief that every place had its own deity. Easily accepted by the Celts was the Roman animalistic belief in the local spirits of hearth, home, family and ancestors. The special Roman contribution to religion in Britain was to provide lasting written and monumental forms to express their own and Celtic gods and religious worship.

Little evidence has come to us about the religion of the Celts from before the Roman occupation. Most of what we know of their worship and deities comes from evidence created by the Romans. Recent research has shown that the Christian religion had a more widespread following in Britain than had previously been thought. The third century martyrs St. Alban, St. Julius and St. Aaron have long been known.

The fact that the Christian Constantine was the Emperor of the part of the Roman empire that included Britain in the fourth century may account for the increasing number of Christian artefacts being found in Britain from this period. Most notable being the earliest set of Christian church plate found at Water Newton.

The Roman Road System

Essential to Roman control of their province of Britain throughout their four centuries of occupation was the system of roads built by the legions using slave and locally conscripted labour throughout the whole island. Built as a military necessity at first they later aided trade and the development of towns and markets, as well as easing the spread of Roman villas all over the countryside.

The roads followed the most easily defendable routes possible and were as straight as the geographical features of the countryside allowed. They can still be identified in modern road atlases, and many main and minor roads still follow their excellent routes. Their construction was and is a feat of civil engineering with excellent surfaces, good drains and extensive use of local materials for their construction being notable features of these roads.

Testimony to their effectiveness is the fact that their actual physical remains can be viewed in most areas of the country to this day. These Roman roads also dictate the position of very many of the towns, villages and settlements of modern Britain. The junction of two Roman roads, the bridging or river crossing points of Roman roads, the hill top sites by Roman roads were sites which the Romans wished to defend either with major army camp sites or minor guard posts. These because of their importance attracted further settlement and thus became population sites which have developed from their Roman origins. Every region of England and Wales has examples of

Background Information for Class Lessons

these settlements which owe their origin to the Roman road engineers. Perhaps the greatest tribute to the Roman road builders can be seen in remote mountainous road sites such as Hardknott pass in the Lake District or Blackstone Edge in the Pennines.

Changes in Later Roman Britain

In the final century before the Romans left the island, Britain witnessed some significant changes. From about 270 A.D. archaeologists notice a considerable growth in construction or enlargement of villas throughout Roman occupied Britain.

Experts in the study of the period have identified the invasion of northern Gaul by barbarians from 276 A.D. as the cause of this expansion in villas. Multiple ownership of villas in neighbouring provinces of the Roman empire meant that a transfer of residence from a ravaged area to an island perceived as being more secure was the main cause of villa building in late third early fourth century Britain. Certainly the large number of villa sites in Northern France show abandonment or burning dating from this time coupled with the lack of reoccupation.

The villa had become an important feature of later Roman Britain with the larger villas of large land - owners being surrounded by clusters of smaller villas of lesser landowners. Most Roman villas in Roman Britain are within ten miles of a town and had a very short lane or private road linking the villa to one of the excellent Roman roads. Archaeologists have identified the final century of Roman rule as a period of reconstruction of town and garrison walls after a long period of neglect. The most notable sites where this occurs are the forts behind Hadrian's Wall and many Northern towns such as York, Chester and Lincoln. This rebuilding was caused by the more frequent raids of the tribes from north of the Wall, and the growing banditry of other tribes south of the wall which had old ties to their northern Celtic neighbours. Towns and Roman settlements along the Channel coasts also see a renewal and extension of their fortifications as the threat of pirate raids becomes more common in the fourth century A.D.

The End of Roman Rule in Britain

The death of Constantine in 337 A.D. meant that the Roman Empire was split in two between his three sons. Each was dissatisfied with this own share of the Empire and warfare between them started in 340 A.D. Britain was under the control of Constantine who used the legions from the island in his campaigns on the continent, severely reducing the military power in Britain for several years. This was at a time when border problems in the north were becoming acute, with the nadir reached in 367 A.D. with Picts, Scots and the northern tribes overrunning northern Britain, and the southern coast being attacked by Franks and Saxons who at the same time over ran northern Gaul. There seems to have been a concerted effort by these disparate raiding tribes to subject Britain to simultaneous attack from as many points of the compass as possible.

Some historians have suggested a conspiracy with detailed information about Roman forces movements and strengths gained from spies within the many Saxons, Franks and Scots used as auxillary troops by the Romans. The Romans at the time called it a conspiracy and the united province of Britain only just survived the combined raids.

The later part of the fourth century was a period when the Roman empire suffered threats from two different sources. First there was internal squabbling within the Roman hierarchy which meant that there was at no time a strong leadership from the centre Rome. Indeed the internal power struggles often meant that one or other of the contestants for power would summon legions from Britain to return to support their power bids in Rome.

Second the Empire was under constant threat from marauding tribes on the eastern, northern and southern boundaries of the Empire. The impact of this on Britain was again that armed forces were frequently summoned from the island to the aid of other threatened provinces. All these demands for help weakened the provinces ability to respond adequately to threats to its own security from both external and internal raiders.

The final stages of Roman control saw different areas of Britain under the control of a variety of warlords or Roman leaders who attempted to hold back invaders from within and without the boundaries of Britain. So even into the fifth century A.D. a rich commander of a region around Gloucester is buried with a grave inscription that suggests he has maintained a Roman style of government for his area whilst surrounded by barbarian invaders.

Another document hints that the Roman commander of the fleet formed to halt pirate raids is in the pay of the Saxon pirates and allows them easy access to the very shores he is meant to protect. Roman Britain slides slowly into anarchy and succumbs region by region to control by raiders from beyond the seas.

Art Ideas on the Theme 'Roman Britain'

Buildings

Teach the children to look out for buildings which show the influence of Roman themes with their pillars, columns, rectangular pediments, and stepped entrances in their local environment.

Research will reveal that the architect of these buildings had paid visits to the sites of Ancient Rome, to study the buildings of the Roman period.

Children will enjoy making scrapbooks of these Roman inspired buildings from press cuttings, brochures and postcards.

Children's drawings of the public buildings, temples and villas of Roman Britain will complement work on shape, symmetry and three-dimensional mathematics. Their drawings will provide good practice in the use of perspective as well as producing excellent displays.

Part of Roman Bath

Tombstones and Decorated Pottery

Much of what we know of the daily life of Roman Britain comes from designs and relief sculpture on the pottery and gravestones that have survived. The relief figures on Roman tombs were painted in bright primary colours. Much of the decorated pottery was Samian ware with black relief figures on a reddy - orange background

Present the children with a variety of blank Roman style pottery and tombstone shapes. Let them use their own research to inspire their figure drawing to fill their blank shapes.

These brightly coloured copies of pottery and tombstones can be displayed as if they were for sale in a Roman Britain pottery shop or mason's yard.

Mosaics

Remnants of Mosaic floors have been found in many Roman Britain sites. They have as their subjects animals, gods and battles. Most mosaics have geometrical borders and often have lettering to explain their content.

Children will enjoy making their own simple copies from scraps cut from brightly coloured magazines, or from gummed coloured paper. Alternatively present the children with a photocopy of a mosaic for them to paint as an exercise in brush and colour control. For a more realistic approach a group of children could work with very small tiles available from DIY suppliers setting them on a plaster base.

Art Ideas on the Theme 'Roman Britain'

Armour and Weapons

Children's research into the different badges and standards of the Roman legions, the variety of shield decoration, armour shapes and patterns will produce dazzling art studies. Their backgrounds should be coloured gold, silver, bronze or other metallic colours, and the features coloured in bright primary colours.

A three-dimensional shield wall could form the background for a display of the children's drawings of the weapons. Children's research could be channelled into making a class room display of a battle between the Celts and the Legions of Roman Britain. The many siege weapons, and ballistic weaponry of the Roman army lend themselves to creative Design Technology modelling using wood, string and waste materials.

Bronze Cavalry Helmet

Borders and Friezes

Many Roman artefacts such as mosaics, urns, vases, and monuments have decorated borders. Children's research will reveal scrolls, geometric and foliage patterns to use as borders symmetrically arranged around their topic work. Contrasting Celtic borders and friezes with interlocking curving patterns, circular designs and animal motifs could be used on the children's work about Roman Britain's native inhabitants.

Frieze depicting Chariot Race

Statues

The Romans had many fine statues of their Emperors, soldiers, gods and goddesses in the forums of their towns and cities. Children should be encouraged to study these fine sculptures and to experiment with their own human figures modelled from clay or plasticine. Chicken wire forms covered with rags soaked in a plaster of Paris mixture is another way of creating sculpture figures.

Plaster casts could be made of the best figures and then modern resin casting components would make a more permanent sculpture.

Bronze depicting the legend of Romulus and Remus

Art Ideas on the Theme 'Roman Britain'

Coins

Children's research in reference books will unearth a wealth of wonderful coins of the various emperors of the Roman occupation of Britain. Children could make clay or plasticine relief copies of these coins which could be painted in gold, silver and bronze.

A classroom time line of children's coin paintings would be an excellent backdrop for the display of other Roman topic work. Replica coins of the Roman era are readily available from a variety of sources. These could be used to produce wax crayon rubbings in metallic colours.

Gladiatorial Combats

The many different attitudes struck by the combatants at these spectacles provide the children with exciting opportunities to study the human body in many different movement poses.

Use a range of different pencil grades or charcoal to shade these black and white copies of the human figure in action.

Wall Paintings

The Romans loved to decorate their rooms with paintings depicting scenes to fit the purpose of the room. Still life of fruit and wine, landscapes, scenes from the legends of their gods and goddesses all were subjects, which have been found in archaeological sites of Roman Britain.

A class project for a large wall painting depicting one of these themes would stimulate large scale drawing and painting among the children. Alternatively groups of children could be designated a room and given the task of providing a wall painting for the room after a period of research for their project.

Three Dimensional Art Work

Three dimensional copies of simple Roman Britain pottery shapes can be made either by the coil method in clay or plasticine. These could be decorated with engraved or relief figures and coloured in reddish brown and black. These shapes will give children experience of 3D work. Plate, vase and bowl shapes made of flat slabs of clay or Plasticine can again have Roman British relief figures applied to them to them. Painted and varnished they will make fine examples of 3D-design work for any school's design technology portfolio.

Ships and the Sea

Roman Britain depended on the sea to sustain its very existence. A class art project could include merchant ships and slave powered galleys full of soldiers sailing through a stormy crossing from Gaul to Britain. The sea could be filled with dolphins, sharks, whales and octopus. Saxon longships with curving sails showing Raven badges, with shields hanging over their side decking could be added to any ship display to show that the decline of Roman Britain came from threat from the sea pirates from the Saxon shores across the North Sea.

Clothes and Jewellery

Let the children make a human figure in card and then drape it in the Roman tunics and togas for the men, and the women in a stolla with a palla draped over it. The clothes can be made from material scraps.

Roman men and women often wore brooches to hold their clothes together . Children could make their own brooches decorated with scraps of coloured foil or similar shiny materials.

The Celtic people wore oval brooches decorated with applied curving coils of metallic wire. Children could make these from card with string glued onto the shapes and scrap beads attached. The whole piece could then be sprayed in a bronze metallic spray. Add a safety pin to the rear and any child could wear this item.

Bracelets formed from plasticine covered in papier-mache can be formed to copy the Celtic curved armlets with their animal headed ends. Again these could be sprayed in a metallic bronze colour. Children could model their bracelets with pride.

Notes for Teachers

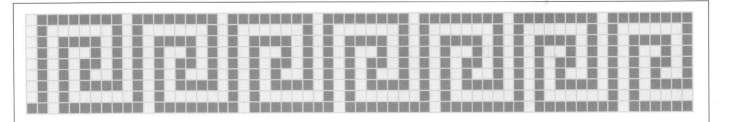

Photocopiable
Worksheets
& Activities

Artefacts Tell Us About the Celts

Some words to help you:
cut, corn, ornament, shield, battle, cook, meals.

Artefact 1

I think that the Celts would

use this to _ _ _ their

_ _ _ _ to make their bread.

I think this because ....

Iron blade

Wooden handle

Artefact 2

torc *n.* (also **torque**) hist. a necklace of twisted metal, esp. of ancient Gaul and Britons.

The torc is flexible and can be pulled apart.

TORC
Eight twisted strands, each of eight wires

I think that this gold and silver item was

used by the Celts as an _ _ _ _ _ _ _ _ .

I think this because ....

Artefact 3

Note the curved Celtic patterns.   77.5cm tall

The Celts would have used this

as a _ _ _ _ _ _ to protect

themselves in _ _ _ _ _ _ .

I think this because ....

Artefact 4

I think that the Celts would use this to

_ _ _ _ their _ _ _ _ _ in.

I think this because.

----

cauldron *n.* (also **caldron**) a large bowl-shaped vessel for boiling over an open fire. [from Latin *caldarium* 'hot bath']

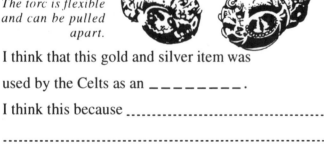

Task B

Research in reference books to find 4 other Celtic artefacts. Carefully draw them, and write about their design, giving your reasons for their use.

Everyday Life in Celtic Britain

Find out about Celtic food from the artefacts they left behind

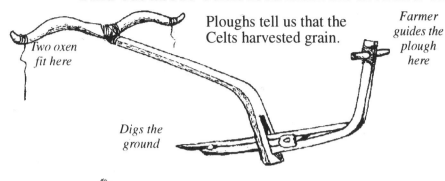

Two oxen fit here

Ploughs tell us that the Celts harvested grain.

Farmer guides the plough here

Digs the ground

Bronze figures of pigs, sheep and cows tell us the Celts ate the meat of these beasts.

A quorn was used for grinding corn.

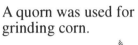

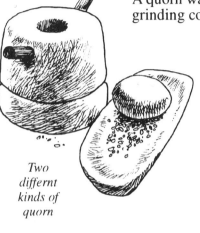

Two differnt kinds of quorn

Ale was made by fermenting barley in storage pits

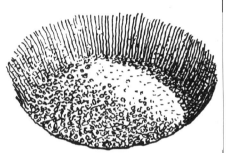

Remains of dome ovens show us how the Celts baked their bread.

Fire-stands tell us that the Celts roasted their meat over their fires.

Large metal cooking pots were used by the Celts to make soup and stews.

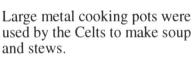

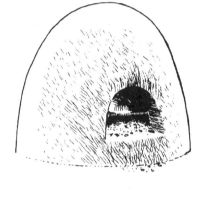

Pots found with the remains of many berry seeds tell us the Celts ate lots of fruit.

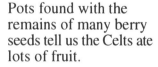

Task - Using Information From Artefacts

1   Draw two large Celtic bronze plates with Celtic patterns around the edges. From your research of the Artefacts above draw two different meals the Celts could have eaten.

2   On a paper plate, make a Celtic meal using Plasticine or clay.

Information Writing Using Different Sources

Artefacts

Archaeologists have found many Celtic objects when they have dug up the site of Celtic settlements.

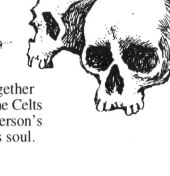

Many skulls found piled together near battle sites tell us that the Celts believed if they captured a person's head, they held the person's soul.

Bronze swords, daggers, and armlets found in lakes and river beds, tell us the Celts sacrificed the goods of their enemies to give thanks for their victory.

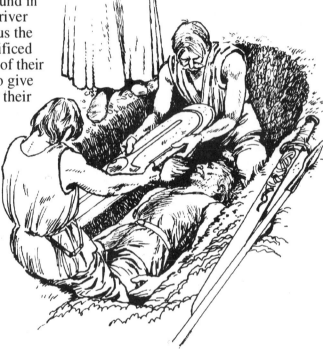

Goods buried with their chiefs show us that the Celts thought they would need to use them in the spirit world. These goods included weapons, clothing, food and cooking utensils.

Written records

Many Roman writers told us about the Druids and the worship of the Celts.

'Their priests are called Druids. They worship in the glades of their forests and by rivers and streams. They sacrifice animals to their Gods under oak trees in the woods. The tribes think their Druids are most powerful'

Paulinus' words, reported by a 1st century A.D. writer.

Task - A Reasoning Exercise

Using different source materials

Study each artefact and each piece of writing carefully, then write down as many things that you have found out about the Celts, and their worship of their Gods, as you can

Make Celtic Symmetry Patterns

From the quarter pattern below copy out 3 repeat patterns
to form your own Celtic symmetrical pattern.

Task B

Now colour your pattern carefully. Use the
Celt's favourite colours of red, green, yellow
and blue.

Task C

Find other Celtic patterns in your reference
books.

The Celts used the interlocking
patterns to show their belief in
all parts of their lives being
woven together. They would
trace the pattern repeatedly
with their fingers, whilst
worshipping their Gods.

The Celts and Nature

A Druid's Harvest Poem

he feast day of Lughnasa,

Is most blessed of all days.

I will swing my sickle in round ways,

I will cut the corn at the full,

Never let my trusty blade be dull,

As the ripe ears from the ground I pull,

Swing my sharp sickle all around,

I take your rich gifts from the ground,

Deep, deep in the earth is your power found.

I swing my bright sickle in round ways,

Lughnasa's is the most blessed of days.

Lug was a legendary Celtic warrior who saved the tribe's harvest from a giant's raid. His feast day (1st August) was called Lughnasa. It marked the start of the harvest for the Celts in Britain. The Druid priests passed down the legend of Lughnasa from one generation to another.

Task A

Research in books for Celtic patterns so that you can carefully draw and colour a border around a piece of A4 sized paper, then in your neatest hand writing copy the poem in the centre of your paper. Finally, learn the Druid's Harvest poem to pass on to other people by reciting it to them.

Task B

Carefully colour the Harvest brooch then try your own twist design for a Celtic brooch on a separate sheet of paper.

All Celtic art has flowing interwoven curves to represent the curves and currents in the streams which the Celts believed carried their God's power through their daily lives.

A Celtic Harvest Brooch

Romans in Britain Timeline

Task A

Cut out each shield and paste it near to the correct place on the Timeline of Roman Britain on the next two pages.

Some of the shields do not have dates. You will have to research their dates from reference books.

Task B

Add further dates and facts to your Timeline as you study Roman Britain.

Julius Caesar lands in Kent and fights the Celts

A.D. 383 British General Magnus Maximus makes himself Emperor

A.D.410 Honourus tells the Britons that Rome can no longer help defend Britain

Forts built to defend the south coast of Britain against Saxon raids A.D. 280

London burned by Boudicca's tribesmen

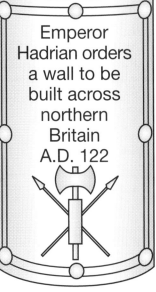

Emperor Hadrian orders a wall to be built across northern Britain A.D. 122

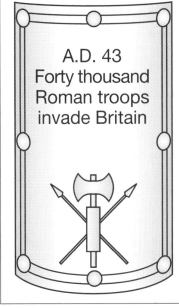

A.D. 43 Forty thousand Roman troops invade Britain

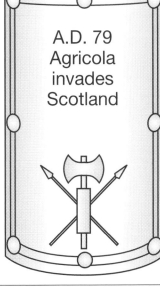

A.D. 79 Agricola invades Scotland

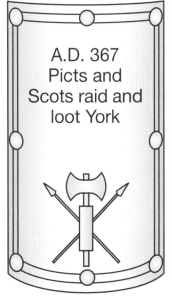

A.D. 367 Picts and Scots raid and loot York

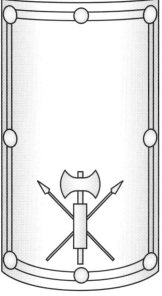

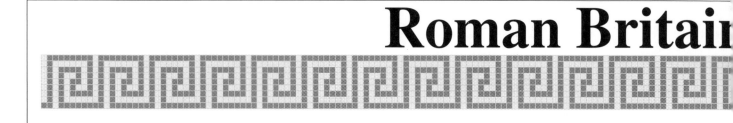

100 B.C.   50 B.C.   0   50 A.D.   100 A.D.   150 A.D.

Time Line

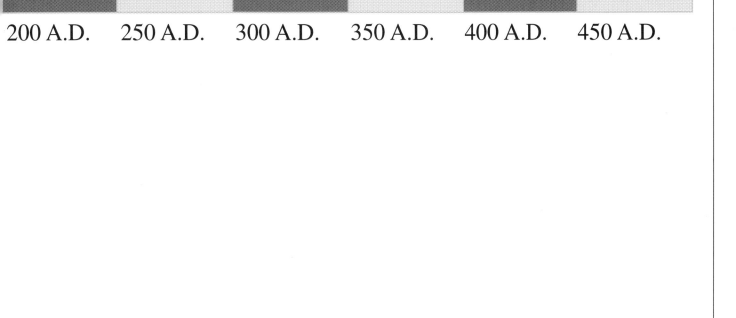

200 A.D.   250 A.D.   300 A.D.   350 A.D.   400 A.D.   450 A.D.

Different Roman Views of Britain

Julius Caesar, writing in 56 B.C. after his short stay in Britain:

"There are many men, buildings and herds of animals. There is much wood. The money is bronze or gold."

Diodorus, writing from Gaul in 30 B.C.:

"Their way of life is simple. There are many people there Much tin is sent from Britain to Gaul."

Tacitus, who lived in Rome and never visited Britain, writing in 86 A.D., after talking to some captives:

"Britain has gold, silver and other metals and pearls."

Solinus, writing in about 200 A.D., never having visited Britain:

"The British do not use money; they get what they want by bartering goods with each other."

Isodorus, writing in Rome, 620 A.D.. He had never been outside Italy:

"Some people think that the Britons are named from the word 'brutes' because they do not have baths and are so far from the main part of the world."

Task A - Interpreting Evidence

Who do you think might have written the sentences below? Look carefully at the evidence before you answer. Put the person's name after you have copied each sentence.

1 "Britons swap instead of buying things with money."

2 "There is lots of tin mined in Britain."

3 "Britain has gold and bronze coins."

4 "The Britons are very dirty."

5 "Pearls are found in the seas around Britain."

Task B - Interpreting Evidence

Answer the following questions in sentences:

1   Why do you think that Tacitus had a better idea about Britain, in Roman times, than Isodorus?

2   Why do you think Diodorus' evidence about Ancient Britain is more reliable than the evidence of Solinus?

3   How do you think that Solinus and Isodorus knew what happened in Britain?

4   Do you think that Solinus and Isodorus had an accurate picture of life in Britain? If not, why do you think this is the case?

Make a Roman Newspaper

On this page you have two news reports plus pictures from your illustrators. Complete the next two pages ready for your newspaper's printing. Cut and paste under your sub-editors suggested titles. Notice that there are some story lines and pictures missing. As print day is tomorrow you will have to research, draw and write these items yourself to fill the empty column space. All the subtitles you need are provided for you.

From Our Reporter With Caesar Fighting in Gaul

Julius Caesar, the brave leader of our armed forces in Gaul, is hopping mad. His fierce fighting forces have no sooner beaten a tribe of Gauls, and taken weapons from them, when the Gauls are sent reinforcements from an island across the seas to the north of Gaul, populated with Celtic tribes related to the Gauls. Our fine General Caesar has let it be known that he will next attack the island people to halt their aid for their kinsmen in Gaul.

Our artist's drawing of the standard bearer of the 10th Legion wading ashore onto the beach in Celtic Britain.

Our artist's impression of the Celtic warriors from the island of Britain.

A Report From Our Tribal Expert

My research has revealed that the island of Britain is filled with mists and fog. These must come from the poisonous nature of the strange island. Reliable sources tell me that the isle is full of rich minerals. Evidence of the rich jewellery worn by the rulers of the Celts in Britain seems to suggest a rich treasure trove for our troops invading Britain, under our wonderful leader Julius Caesar. Further information from captured Celts fighting our troops in Gaul suggest that the island called Britain is full of strange and fierce monsters which dwell in the forests of the island.

ROMAN TIMES

Available monthly - September 55B.C.

Price III denarii

Britain Full of Monsters and Poison

Caesar Hopping Mad as Britons Aid Gaul

British Warriors Wait on the Beaches

Britons Fight in Blue Paint

ROMAN TIMES

Available monthly - September 55 B.C.

Price III denarii

Standard Bearer Leaps Into Sea and Saves Day for Caesar

Celtic Warrior Tells of Beach Fight

....
....
....
....
....
....
....
....
....

Soldier of 'Tenth' Tells of Beach Battle

....
....
....
....
....
....
....
....

Roman Ships Wrecked in Gale

Roman Retreat - Caesar Promises to Return

....
....
....
....
....
....
....

Battling Boudicca

Task - A Character Study of Celtic Britain's Most Famous Woman

Research in reference books to find out as much information as you can about Boudicca, then continue the character sketch of Boudicca which has been started for you here...

Boudicca was used to ordering people about. As a princess in the Celtic tribe called the Iceni, she would have many servants ready to follow her every wish.

Continue on the back of the sheet if necessary.

A Roman Soldier's Kit

By each piece of Roman soldier's kit write three or more sentences about what the kit is made of, what it is used for and why you think it was important to the Roman soldier.

Research in reference books to help you find more information about the Roman Soldier's kit. The first one has been done for you.

Basic Clothes

The Roman soldier wore a short sleeved tunic made of wool for cold places, and cotton for hot places. They wore knee length leather pants to protect their limbs from thorns or from sword blows in battle. On top of their pants they wore a short kilt like skirt. This kept them warm but allowed them to move easily.

The shield is made from wooden strips, covered in leather, with metal strengthening.

The Helmet

The Spear

The Mortarium

The Axe

The Spade

Camping - Roman Army Style

Fact 1
The Roman army, on a long march, would choose a hilltop to camp on, so that the sentries could see for long distances.

Fact 2
The Roman soldiers would dig a ditch round their camp to make attack difficult.

Fact 3
The Roman army would make a 2 metre high fence around their camp, from small trees cut down by the soldiers. This would help stop attack.

Fact 4
Eight soldiers would share a canvas tent. They would roll it up over the tent poles and carry it between two men.

Fact 5
Each group of eight men, called contubernium (tent) would carry a mortarium to grind their corn for their bread, which they could cook over the fire.

Fact 6
Each contubernium would carry a tripod, cooking bowls and cooking implements hanging from a spear between two men.

Task - Explanatory Letter Writing

Imagine you are a Roman soldier on a long march and you have set up camp for the night. Write an imaginary letter, back to your family in Italy, telling them exactly how you set up camp with your men. Use the facts and pictures to help you.

Roman Baths

Lucius Seneca A.D 63

"I live above the Public Baths in our town - you can guess what that means. Ugh ! It's dreadful. First there are 'fitness fanatics' doing their exercises and swinging heavy weights about with loud grunts and groans. Then there are the lazy ones having a cheap massage. I can hear the slaps of the masseurs on their fat bodies. Then there is always someone who loves the sound of his own voice shouting his opinions from the hot room. And finally there are always plenty who have to make a huge splash and scream when they jump into the cold bath."

Lucian, writing in his 'Satires'

"When you enter the baths there is a large hall with massage rooms and rooms for the bath slaves and attendants...then there are rooms to undress in... next you walk into a slightly warmed room to prepare you for the fierce heat of the next room - the hot room with its steamy atmosphere. Then there are the hot tubs, where you can soak in comfort. When you have bathed you walk through into the cold room to rest. Afterwards you can sit or exercise in the courtyard outside."

Tepidarium

A warm room with benches for people to sit on whilst they get used to the heat.

Laconicum

A hot, but very dry room, with benches where you can dry off.

Palaestre

A courtyard where people can exercise or sit on benches under a veranda for shade.

Caldarium

A hot and steamy room, with very hot baths sunk into the floor.

Hypocaust

An underground heating system, where hot air from a furnace is driven under the rooms.

Task - Using Information From Different Sources

1   Carefully study the text and the picture above and then make an A4 sized poster advertising a Roman Bath. Make sure you list all the attractions and features.

2   Divide a piece of paper down its length. On one side list the facilities of the Roman Baths and on the other side list the facilities of your nearest modern leisure centre.

Taking it further

Compare the passage by Lucius Seneca with the passage written by Lucian. Make a list of the good and bad points about Roman Baths. Which writer is in favour or the baths and which is not in favour of the baths?

Make a Roman Mosaic

Task A - Writing Instructions

Carefully study the pictures and text below about how to make your own Roman mosaic. Write your own simple instructions to fill in the missing spaces.

1

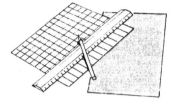

Using a ruler and pencil, divide different coloured pieces of paper into 1cm squares. You will have to decide how many colours you want to use in your mosaic.

2

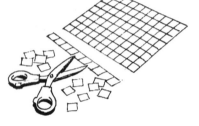

3

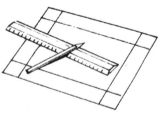

On a piece of A4 white paper, draw a frame 3cm wide around the edge of the paper.

4

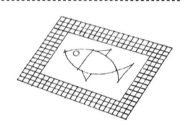

5

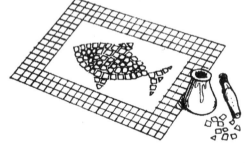

Draw your own simple design in the centre of your A4 piece of paper.

6

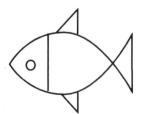

Task B

Now follow your instructions and make your own Roman mosaic. Use these designs to help you.

Rules for: The Legions on the March Game

A Game for up to 4 Players

How to play the game

1 Throw the dice to see who plays first.

2 Each choose a Legion symbol.

3 Each player collects a set of 5 Order Cards. Shuffle and then place them face down on your desk.

4 Each player collects a Route Note Sheet.

5 Each player in turn takes an Order Card from the top of their pile. Start with your Legion symbol on Lundinium. Throw the dice and move the number of places along the route to your destination.

6 Any order along the way must be observed.

7 As the player moves they must note down on their own Route Note Sheet the Roman towns and the Celtic tribal lands they pass through.

8 When the player arrives at their destination, they return their symbol to Londinium, await their next turn, pick up their next Order Card, then follow the route.

9 The game ends when the first player has completed all their routes and written up their Route Note Sheets.

10 In the event of a tie the best Route Note Sheet, judged by the teacher, will decide the winner.

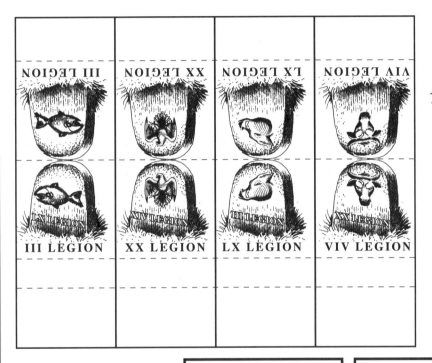

Cut out the milestones and fold as shown in the illustration. Fix with glue.

1
March to Vinlandia to defend the wall from attack by the Valadini tribe.

2
March to Dubris to help defend the port from Saxon pirate raids.

Order Cards

5
March to Isca to help put down a mutiny by the fort's auxiliary troops.

4
Your Legion is ordered to Aqua Sulis for a rest period at the healing waters.

3
March to Deva to defend the city from raids by the wild Brigantes tribe.

Route Note Sheet

Roman Towns Visited with their Modern Names:

Celtic Tribal Lands Visited:

The Legions on the March Game

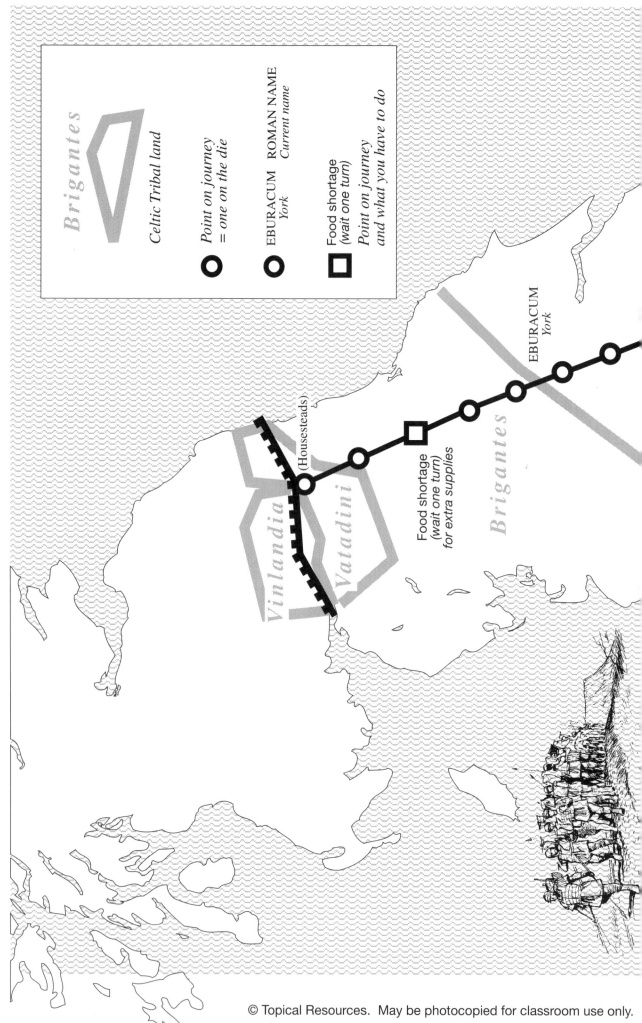

Brigantes

Celtic Tribal land

⬤ Point on journey = one on the die

◎ EBURACUM ROMAN NAME
York Current name

▢ Food shortage (wait one turn)
Point on journey and what you have to do

(Housesteads)

Vinlandia

Vatadini

Brigantes

EBURACUM
York

Food shortage (wait one turn) for extra supplies

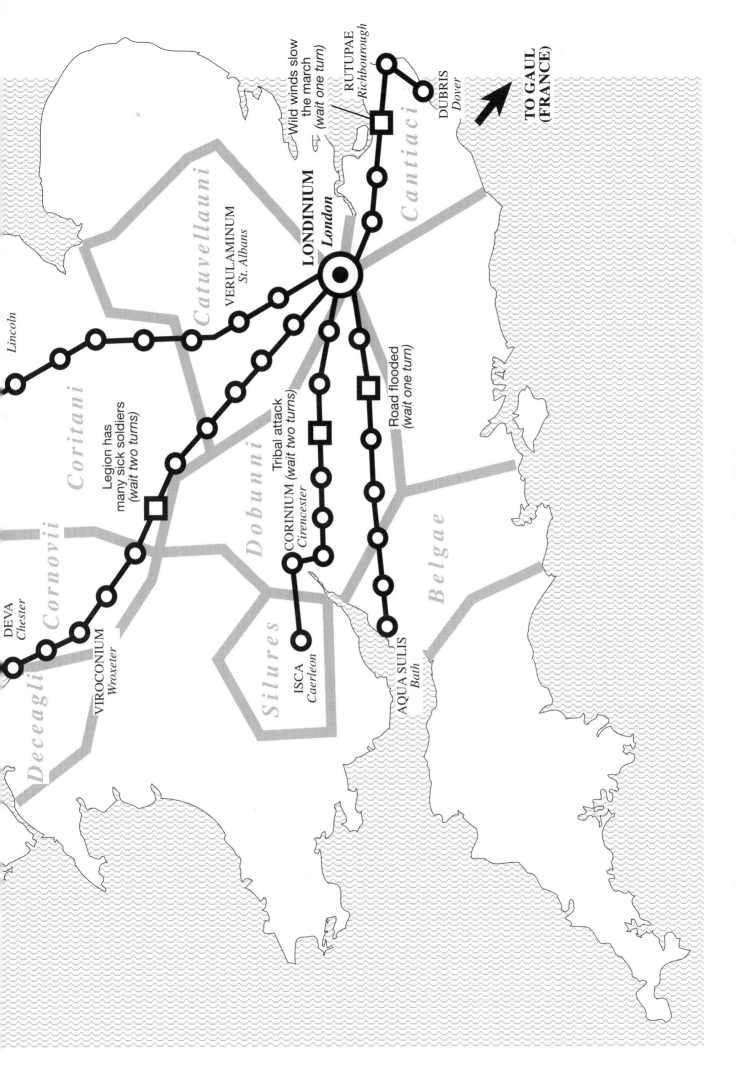

TO GAUL
(FRANCE)

RUTUPAE
Richbourough

DUBRIS
Dover

Wild winds slow
the march
(wait one turn)

LONDINIUM
London

Cantiaci

VERULAMINUM
St. Albans

Catuvellauni

Lincoln

Coritani

Legion has
many sick soldiers
(wait two turns)

Dobunni

Tribal attack

CORINIUM *(wait two turns)*
Cirencester

Road flooded
(wait one turn)

Belgae

Deceagli

Cornovii

DEVA
Chester

VIROCONIUM
Wroxeter

Silures

ISCA
Caerleon

AQUA SULIS
Bath

Information From Roman Artefacts

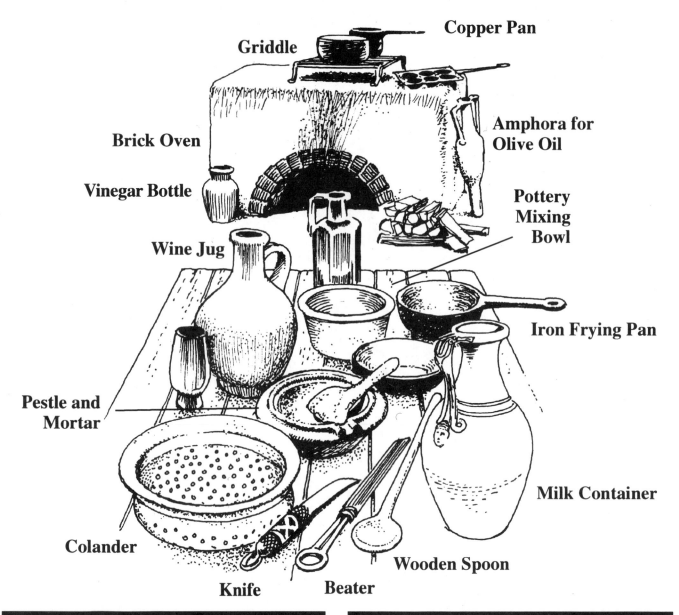

Copper Pan
Griddle
Brick Oven
Amphora for Olive Oil
Vinegar Bottle
Pottery Mixing Bowl
Wine Jug
Iron Frying Pan
Pestle and Mortar
Milk Container
Colander
Wooden Spoon
Knife
Beater

Task A

Study the picture of Roman kitchen artefacts:

1   List the artefacts which were used to prepare food for cooking.

2   List the artefacts the Romans used to cook with.

3   List the artefacts used for holding liquids.

4   What fuel do you think the Romans used to provide heat for their cooking?

Task B

List the utensils used in your home for preparing food, cooking food and the fuel used to heat your meals.

Do we still use any kitchen items that are similar to those the Romans used two thousand years ago?

Name some of them.

Food in Roman Britain

Incentaculum

The Romans would start the day with a light-meal of bread and fruit. They loved figs, dates and grapes. Romans living in Britain would eat only dried versions of these fruits. It would be more normal for Romans living in Britain to eat apples, pears, plums and other soft fruits at their first meal of the day.

Prandium

The Romans would eat a light meal at midday. At this meal they would have cooked meats such as chicken, lamb, beef or fish, with salad vegetables and bread.

Cena

The main meal for the Romans was eaten about 4 o'clock in the afternoon. It had three main courses:- **Gustatio** (a taster of a variety of dishes made from egg, fish or vegetables), **Prima Mensae** (the main course of meat and vegetables and **Secundae Mensae** (sweet dishes or fruits).

Roman Recipes

Stuffed Dormouse
Stuff the dormouse with chopped pork, pepper, ginger and cloves.

Bake in a hot oven.

Snails in Garlic
Boil the snails until tender with chopped garlic.

Chicken stuffed with Liquamen
Mix a paste of dried fish, oregano, thyme, and pepper. Stuff the chicken with this. Bake in a hot oven. Serve with boiled onions and leeks.

Honeyed Bread
Break some old bread into large pieces, soak in milk. Fry in Honey, then roll in crushed pine nuts.

Gruel
Boil wheat or barley in milk. Serve with honey.

Spiced Sausages
Chop up pork and beef, mix with pepper, salt, and garlic. Fill a pig's intestine with the mixture. Grill and serve with boiled cabbage.

Stuffed Chicken
Chop up onions, garlic, thyme and rosemary. Mix with wine and pine kernels. Stuff the chicken with this mixture. Bake in a hot oven and serve with boiled beans.

Oysters in Wine
Boil the oysters in wine with chopped onions. Serve on a flat bread.

Squid in sauce
Chop the squid in small pieces. Fry fennel,, cardomen and coriander in olive oil. Add the squid and fry until cooked.

Stuffed Dates
Take the stones out of the dates and fill with nutmeg and cloves and honey.

Sweets
Boil wheat in milk until it becomes a paste. Cool and cut into cubes. Serve covered in honey.

Stew
Boil onions, garlic, cabbage and beans with salt, pepper and herbs. Serve with bread.

Task - A Reasoning Exercise

1 Using the information above, make up a day's menu card for a Roman family.

2 Conduct a survey of your class or friends to find their Top Ten favourite Roman recipes.

Be an Archaeologist on a Roman Road Site

A recent report in the Lincoln Times newspaper.

Jane Trowel's Reconstruction Drawings of a Roman Road Made After Evacuations South of Lincoln

Builders working on the site of a new housing development, south of the city, have been forced to halt work after the discovery of what may prove to be an important Roman find. Our reporter interviewed the County Archaeologist Mr. E. Digger, who stated that with the help of students at Nottingham University, he hopes to reveal the longest section of Roman road ever found in good condition in Britain.

Bedding Pebbles

Irregular pebbles from local streams from 3 to 5 cm in diameter, packed tightly together. Top layer showing signs of flattening mallet.
Pebbles used to provide a flat surface.

Draining Base Stones

Large pebbles from the bed of a local stream used to form easy draining under the road. Irregular size and shape.

Flattened Earth

Curved marks on the surface of the earth under the base stones show Romans had curved spades.

Surface Stones

Large stone cut into irregular 10 to 12 cm slabs. Chisel marks show the efforts to make a flat surface.

Ditch Flags

Found 10 cm below the edge of the road. Square shaped 12cm by 12 cm. Chisel marks on all surfaces.

Task - A Reasoning Exercise

1. What evidence tells you that the Romans wanted a flat surface to their roads?
2. Why do you think the Romans put large stones at the base of their roads?
3. What evidence tells you that the Romans made use of local streams?
4. Why do you think the Romans made a sunken ditch at either side of their roads?
5. List the tools the Romans used to make their roads.
6. Why do you think the Romans wanted a flat surface to their roads?
7. Why do you think the Romans used a bed of small pebbles just below the surface of their roads?
8. Why do you think the Romans took such care building good roads?

Taking it further:

Research in reference books to find out other equipment the Romans used to build their roads.

Ships -The Lifeline of Roman Britain

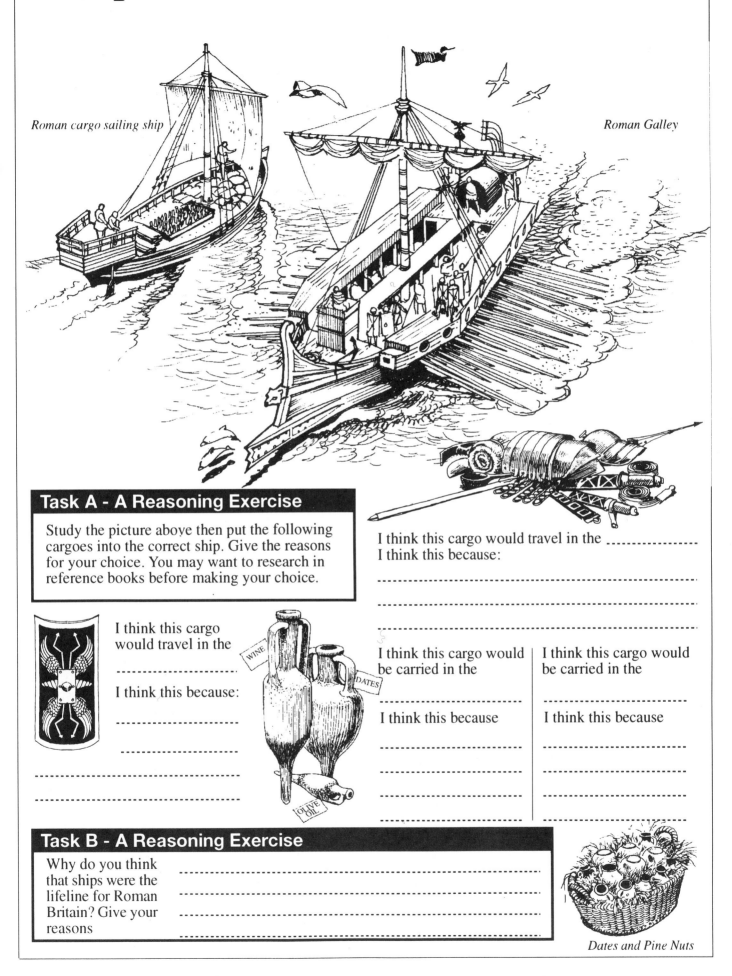

Roman cargo sailing ship

Roman Galley

Task A - A Reasoning Exercise

Study the picture above then put the following cargoes into the correct ship. Give the reasons for your choice. You may want to research in reference books before making your choice.

I think this cargo would travel in the ....
I think this because:

I think this cargo would travel in the

I think this because:

WINE

DATES

OLIVE OIL

I think this cargo would be carried in the

I think this because

I think this cargo would be carried in the

I think this because

Task B - A Reasoning Exercise

Why do you think that ships were the lifeline for Roman Britain? Give your reasons

----

Dates and Pine Nuts

Instruction For Making Roman Models

To make all the models larger use your photocopier to reproduce the pages onto A3 card.

Before you start to assemble your Roman Models research in books to find the appropriate colours. Colour all pieces with pencil crayons, felt tip pens or paints before you cut anything out.

Roman Galley

1. Cut out all pieces along solid black lines.
2. Score along all dotted lines.
3. Fold base plate as shown on Diagram 1.
4. Fold bow and stern pieces as shown in Diagram 2, paste into shape
5. Paste side pieces to base flaps A, B, C, D, E and F.
6. Fold decking piece as shown on Diagram 3. Paste centre section of decking piece to base. Paste flaps G and H under base plate through gaps in the base plate.
7. Paste flaps I, J, K and L under decking.
8. Paste bow piece to the inside of ship with flaps M and N. Paste flap O to base plate. Paste stern piece to side of ship with flaps P and Q. Paste flap R to base plate.
9. Paste mast piece into place as shown in Diagram 4. Alternatively, use an art straw, or piece of dowel.
10. Paste flaps S and T on sail piece to side decking as shown in Diagram 4. Paste top of sail to mast.
11. Paste Shelter flaps V and W to stern deck as shown in Diagram 4.

Roman Villa

1. Cut out 4 House shapes. Score along all dotted lines.
2. Fold gable ends in and base up. Paste flaps E and F to base, as shown in Diagram a.
3. Fold roof piece over. Paste flaps A, B,C and D to inside of roof, as shown in Diagram b. Fold inside wall piece over. Paste flaps G and H to inside of gable ends.
4. Paste flaps J, K and I to inside of shape, as shown in Diagram c. Repeat 2 - 4 above to make 4 houses.
5. Cut out 4 Inner Veranda pieces from page 42. Score along all dotted lines. Paste flap H under hatched section

and fold flaps M and L inwards. Paste hatched part of Veranda to hatched part of two houses only. Call these houses 3 and 4.
6. Cut out and score dotted lines to make two outer Outer Verandas (on page 42.) Fold as in Diagram d, and paste flap P to back of inner wall. Fold flaps Q and R under. Fold front section so that flaps S and T can be pasted at T and S on roof of veranda. Cut sections away to make a left hand and right hand Outer Veranda.(See Daigram d on page 42 to help you.)
7. Cut out and score dotted lines of Porch shape. Paste flap Y onto floor of the outer veranda and flap V on the floor of the other veranda to join outer verandas together.

Assembly of Villa on Courtyard Base

1. Paste Houses with their fronts aligned with line at edge of courtyard. (Make sure houses 3 and 4 go in the correct places.) As you paste each house in position, paste art straw as pillars to the underside of the the veranda and to the courtyard base.
2. Glue one inner veranda across fronts of houses 1 and 2.
3. Use extra roof pieces to fill gaps between corner houses. (See drawing of Roman Villa.)
4. Paste outer veranda and porch to its place on the courtyard base. Paste outer veranda to the gable ends of houses 3 and 4.
5. Glue remaining inner veranda to rear of porch.

Roman Soldier's Helmet

1. Cut out all sections of the helmet. Score along all dotted lines. Fold creases with great care.
2. As you build each part check with the diagram on page 40.
3. Paste part A so that the shaded part is covered by the flap and the arrows are aligned.
4. Paste part B so that the arrows are aligned.
6. Paste part A to top tabs on part B.
7. Paste shaded tab on part C1 to part C2 and C2 tab to part C1. Put a pencil mark L and R over the ear spaces and an F to indicate front of the Helmet.
8. Paste part C tabs to bottom of part

A/B, to form crown of the Helmet.
9. Starting behind left ear space, paste tabs on part E (neck guard) to the back of the helmet in such a way as the last tab fits behind the right ear space.
10. Paste part F (Visor) at front of Helmet making sure it lines up with the curves in front of the left and right ear spaces.
11. Fold part D and paste folded V shape into hole at top Helmet and curved base to curve behind the ear spaces at each side.
12. Paste pommel to centre top of Helmet, to complete your model. Cut strips of coloured paper to form a plume which you can paste to the top of the pommel.

Hadrian's Wall

Arched Gateway (page 49)

1. Cut out Gatehouse shape, score & fold all dotted lines.
2. Carefully fold as shown in Diagram A.
3. Glue flaps to assemble the model as shown in Diagram B.

Upper Floor (page 50)

4. Cut out Upper Floor Shape. Score and fold along dotted lines.
5. Assemble as shown in Diagram C.

Rampart (page 50)

6. Cut out Rampart shapes. Score and fold along dotted lines.
7. Assemble as shown in Diagram D

Wall Section (page 51)

8. Cut out Wall Section shape. Score and fold along dotted lines.
9. Assemble as shown in Diagram E.

Assembly

By mass producing the above components a section of Hadrian's Wall which includes simple Mile Castles and Signal Turrets can now be built. (See Diagrams E, F and G.)

Hadrian's Wall was built after the Emperor Hadrian had visited Britain in 122 A.D. It stretched from coast to coast a distance of 73 miles. It took about eleven years to build and used half a million metric tonnes of stone. It had seventeen forts along its length, with Mile castles every thousand paces and signalling turrets between every Mile castle . On the northern side it had a deep defensive ditch, and on the southern side a wider ditch with a road running the full length of the wall. The wall was garrisoned by 5,500 cavalry and 13,000 infantry troops.

Roman Galley

Instructions are on page 38

You will need scissors, ruler, pencil, crayons and glue

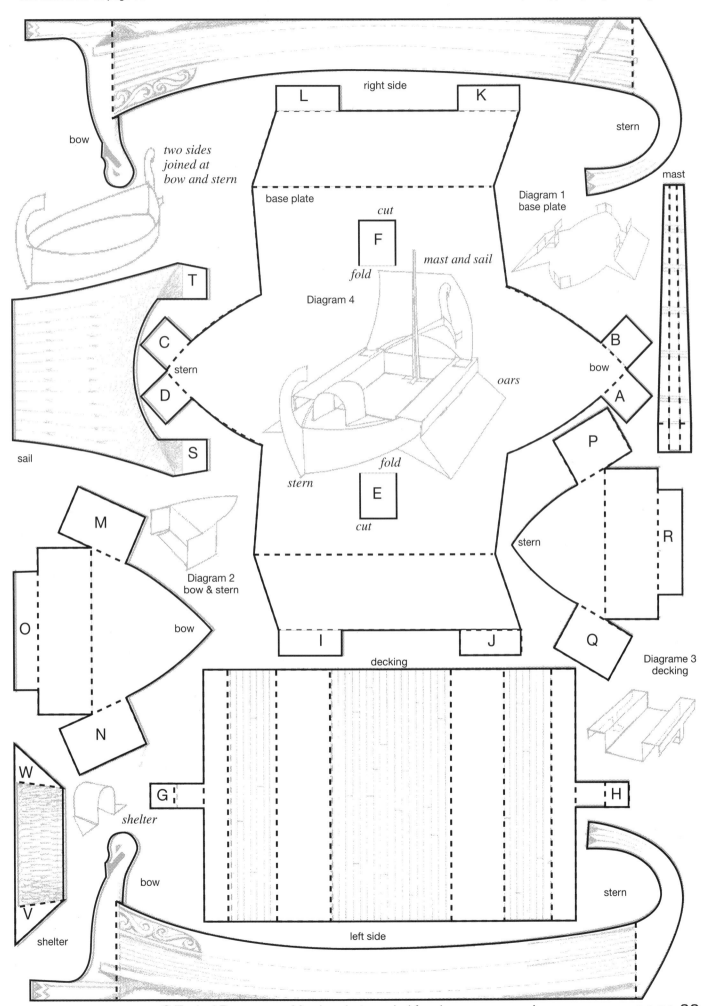

bow

*two sides
joined at
bow and stern*

right side

L K

stern

base plate

Diagram 1
base plate

mast

cut

F

mast and sail

fold

Diagram 4

B

bow

A

oars

P

T

C

stern

D

S

fold

E

cut

stern

R

sail

Q

M

Diagram 2
bow & stern

bow

Diagrame 3
decking

O

decking

N

I J

shelter

G

H

W

bow

stern

V

shelter

left side

Roman Helmet

Instructions are on page 38

You will need scissors, ruler, pencil, crayons and glue.

part A

cut

cut out

part B

E - neck guard

pommel

front

back

F - Visor and cheek guards

left ear

part D

1

2

6

3

4

5

back

front

part C1

part C2

right ear

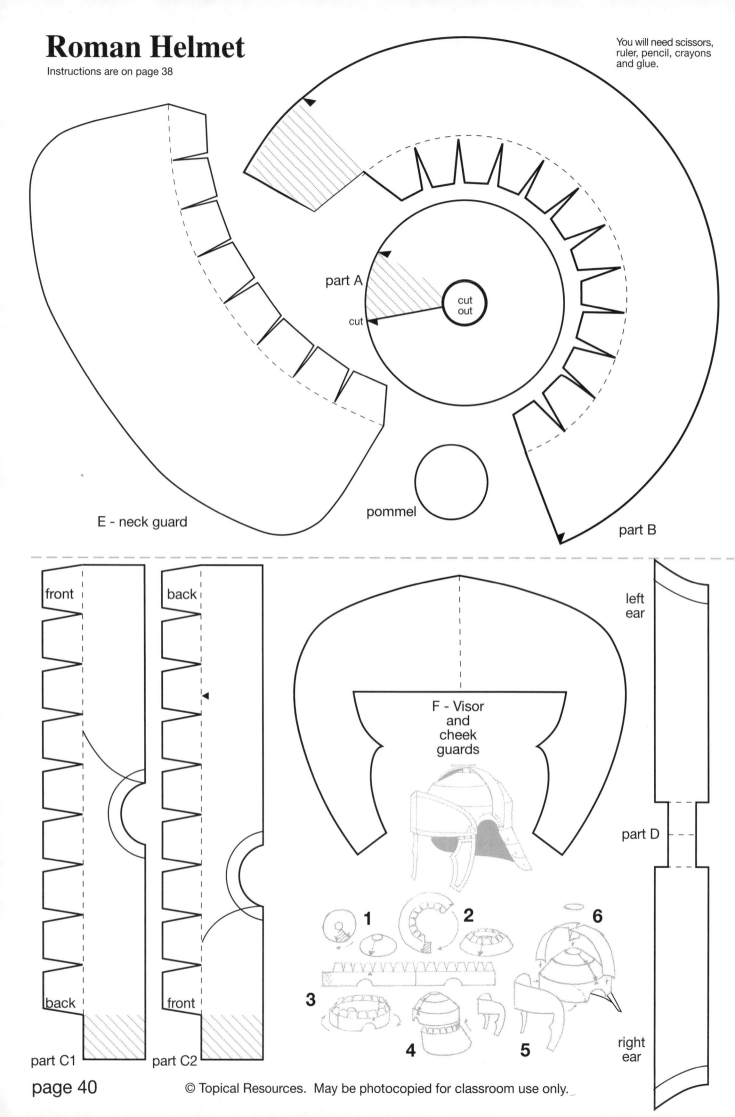

Roman Villa

Instructions are on page 38

You will need scissors, ruler, pencil, crayons and glue

You will need four of these house units to make one villa

Diagram a

Diagram b

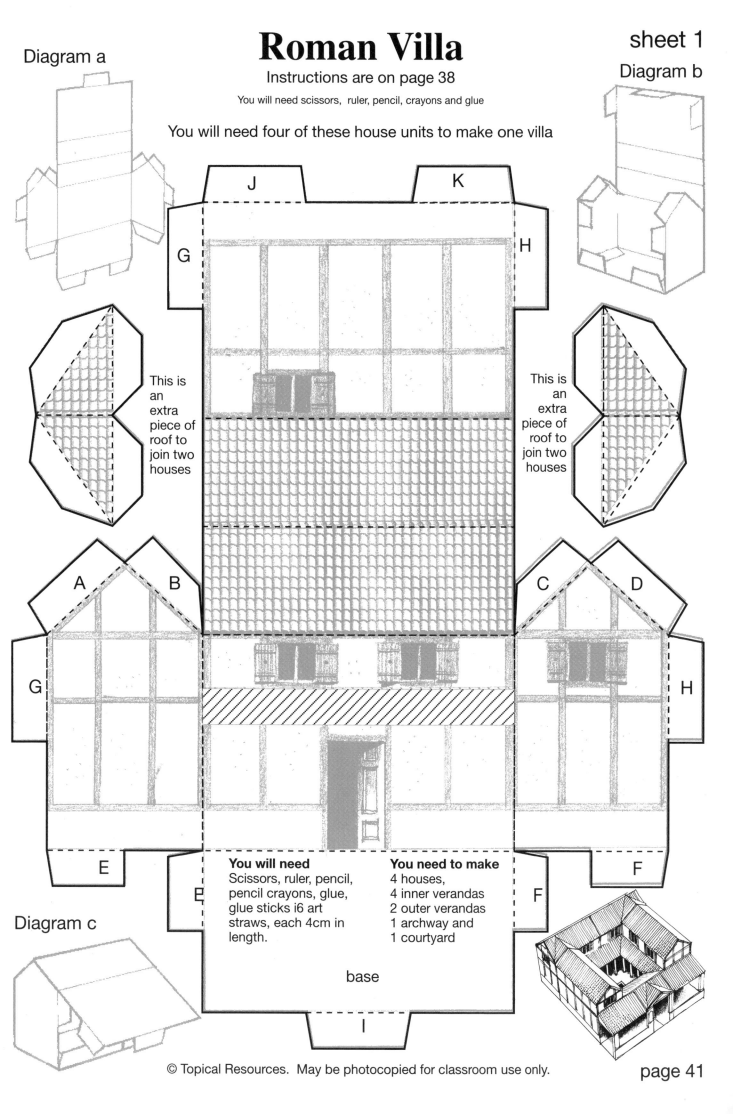

This is an extra piece of roof to join two houses

This is an extra piece of roof to join two houses

J   K

G   H

A   B   C   D

G   H

E   F

E   F

You will need
Scissors, ruler, pencil, pencil crayons, glue, glue sticks i6 art straws, each 4cm in length.

You need to make
4 houses,
4 inner verandas
2 outer verandas
1 archway and
1 courtyard

base

I

Diagram c

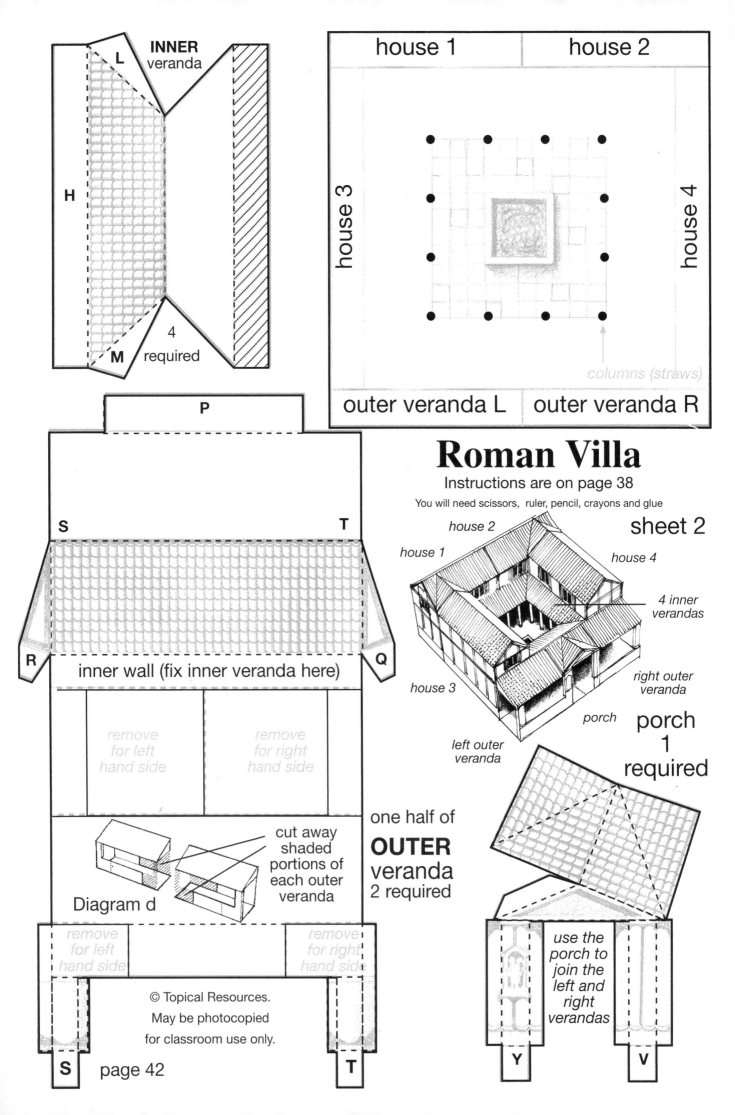

INNER veranda

L

H

M

4 required

house 1   house 2

house 3

house 4

columns (straws)

outer veranda L   outer veranda R

P

S   T

R   Q

inner wall (fix inner veranda here)

remove for left hand side   *remove for right hand side*

cut away shaded portions of each outer veranda

Diagram d

one half of **OUTER** veranda 2 required

remove for left hand side   *remove for right hand side*

S   page 42   T

Roman Villa

Instructions are on page 38

You will need scissors, ruler, pencil, crayons and glue

house 2
house 1   sheet 2
house 4

4 inner verandas

house 3

right outer veranda

porch   porch 1 required

left outer veranda

use the porch to join the left and right verandas

Y   V

The Roman Gods and Goddesses

Evidence From Stone Remains

Many Roman House Shrines made of stone have been discovered throughout Britain. Close examination of the remains show traces of red, yellow, blue, green and gold paint on the stones. The statues must have provided bright centres of worship throughout the houses of Roman Britain.

A house shrine of the God Janus, who is looking in two directions to guard the main house door.

An inscription carved on a Roman house shrine. It is written in the Roman language and says 'Mithras gives light to our home with thanks'.

Evidence on Inscriptions on Stone Remains

Vesta — was the goddess of the hearth or fire.

The Penates — were the spirits who guarded the storeroom.

Janus — was the god who protected the main door.

Mithras — was the Persian god who the Romans used as a god of light in their homes.

Evidence From the Remains of Buildings

Archaeologists are able to look at the foundations of Roman Temples and the stone remains of part of the Temples and then draw accurate pictures of what the Temple would have been like.

Here is an artist's impression of what the Temple of Sul Minerva must have looked like in Roman times.

Sul Minerva was the Roman Goddess of healing. Her temple was built over the natural spring in Bath which the Romans believed could cure many illnesses.

Task - Interpreting Evidence From Different Sources

Carefully read the statements below and from the evidence above decide whether each statement is **true** or **false** or **there is no evidence** for you to decide. Write a reason for your choice to go with each statement.

1   Roman shrines were made of wood.
2   Roman house shrines were originally brightly painted.
3   Archaeologists found traces of paint on Roman house shrines.
4   Thousands of Roman house shrines have been dug up by archaeologists.
5   Archaeologists know a lot about Roman gods because Julius Caesar told them.
6   Janus is a Roman door god.
7   Roman homes were very dark so Mithras gave them light.
8   Archaeologists use the remains of buildings to help them draw pictures of Roman Temples.
9   Some Roman gods had springs of water named after them.
10   The Romans sacrificed sheep and goats to their gods.

The Emperor Claudius Comes to Britain

Task A - Biographical Writing

The facts about the Emperor Claudius below have been mixed up. Cut them out and paste them into the correct order on a fresh piece of paper.

A.D. 43 Claudius orders 40,000 Roman troops to invade Britain to put down the revolt of Caractacus, a British tribal king.

From A.D. 49 to 54 Claudius' nephew, the mad and cruel Emperor Caligula often had Claudius thrown into the river Tiber in Rome, at night, as a joke.

10 B.C. Claudius was born in Lugdunum, Gaul. He is a weak and sickly child.

Task B - Biographical Writing

Research in refence books to write a short biography of Julius Caesar.

A.D. 43 After the battle of Medway, Claudius spends 16 days in Britain, leading his troops into Colchester.

Claudius, who prefers books to the army or helping to rule Rome, writes his history of early Rome, 20 to 34 A.D.

Soldiers kill the Emperor Caligula and vote for Claudius as their emperor A.D.41

Claudius is poisoned by his fourth wife, Aggrippina and Nero succeeds him as emperor in

The Gladiators

Make your own pop up Roman Gladiators Amphitheate and entertain the troops at a Roman fort

Instructions

1 Copy pages 45, 46, and 47 onto thin card.
2 Use masking tape to join pages 46 and 47 together.
3 Research in reference books to find pictures of Roman Soldiers and gladiators, then carefully colour the figures A, B, C and D on this page, and the background Amphitheatre on pages 46/47.

4 Cut out around the shapes A, B, C and D and fold to form front and back of figure on a stand.
5 Place your figures in the arena to face each other in combat and prop up the background scenery.
6 Write your own report of an imaginary Roman Gladiators' contest in your amphitheatre in the space provided on page 47.

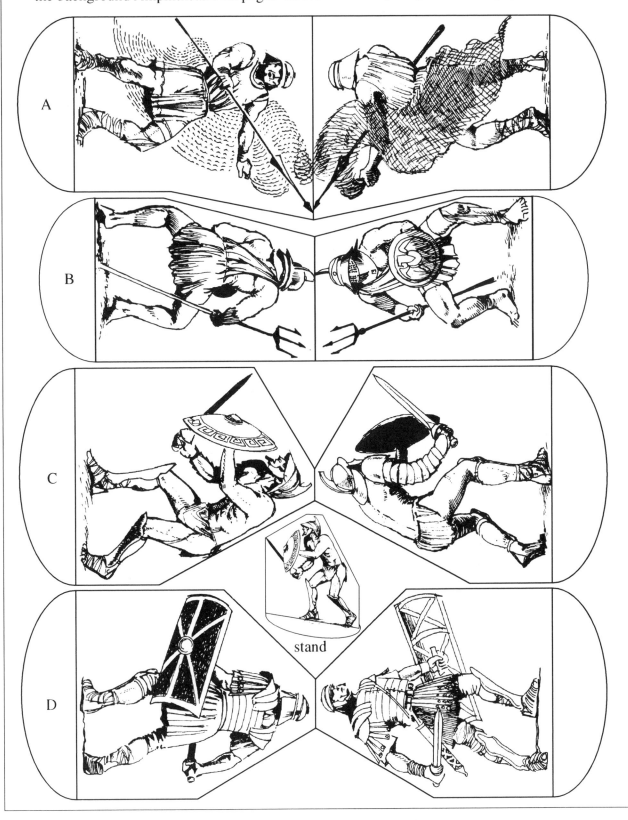

stand

The Gladiators in the Amphitheatre

© Topical Resources. May be photocopied for classroom use only.

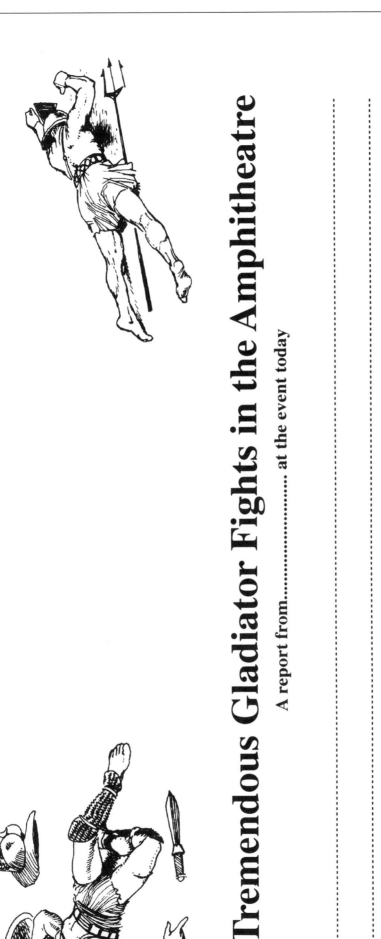

Tremendous Gladiator Fights in the Amphitheatre

A report from................ at the event today

- -

- -

- -

- -

- -

- -

- -

Study Different Views About Hadrian's Wall

Emperor Hadrian

Scotinus the Pict

Task A - Understanding That There are Different Views of the Same Event

Carefully read the statements below. Think about who might have made these comments, either the Roman Emperor Hadrian, or the Pict leader, Scotinus. Cut each statement out and paste it under the correct leader on your own sheet.

Statements

1 The wall will keep out the wild northern tribes.

2 A wall can easily be climbed. It won't stop my men.

3 The best time to attack will be on foggy winter nights.

4 We can watch out for the spot where there are least Romans, then attack.

5 I have designed the wall so that soldiers can rest in safe places every mile, but be ready to rush to fight off any attack.

6 They will need lots of men to make the wall safe, and their soldiers will not like our northern weather.

7 My reason for building the wall was to stop the damage the Pict tribes were doing to our towns in northern Britannia.

8 With well made roads along the southern side of the wall, I can move troops from one trouble spot to another.

9 You can easily signal from one mile castle to another to warn of any danger.

10 We have not captured as much Roman gold and jewels as we used to get on our raids.

Task B - Describing Different Views of the Same Event

Imagine an attack on Hadrian's wall by the Pict tribes from the north.

Write a Roman soldier's view of the attack, then a Pict warrior's view of the same attack on the wall.

Hadrian's Wall

Instructions are
on page 38

base

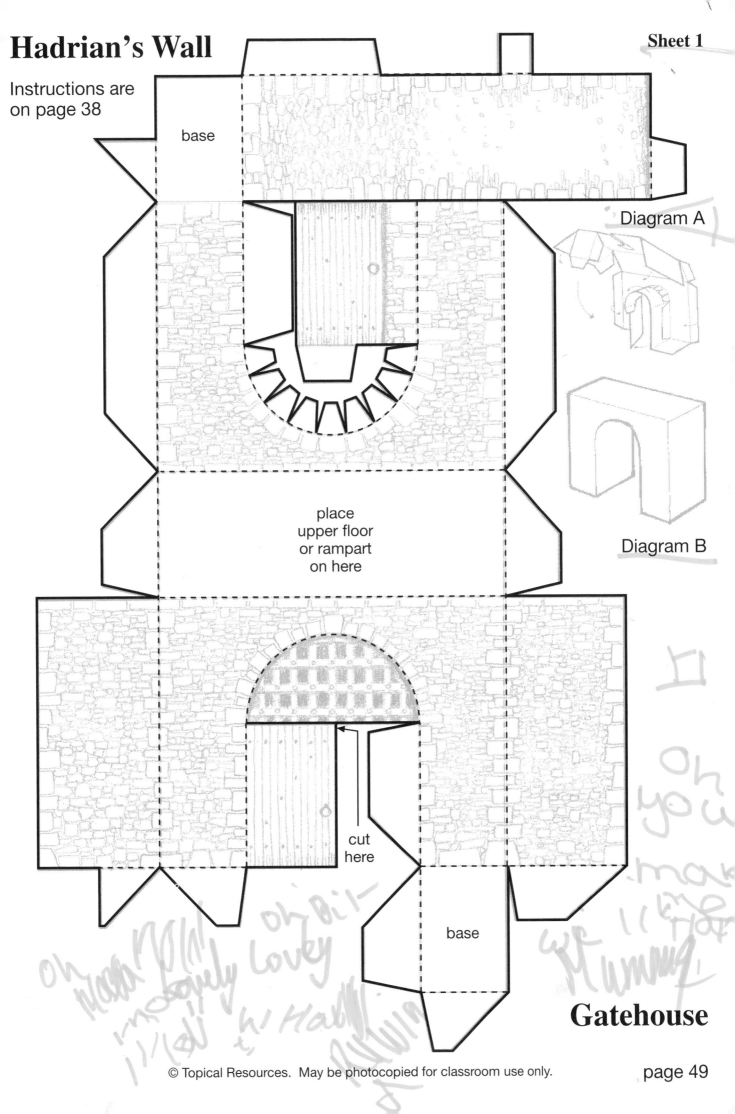

Diagram A

place
upper floor
or rampart
on here

Diagram B

cut
here

base

Gatehouse

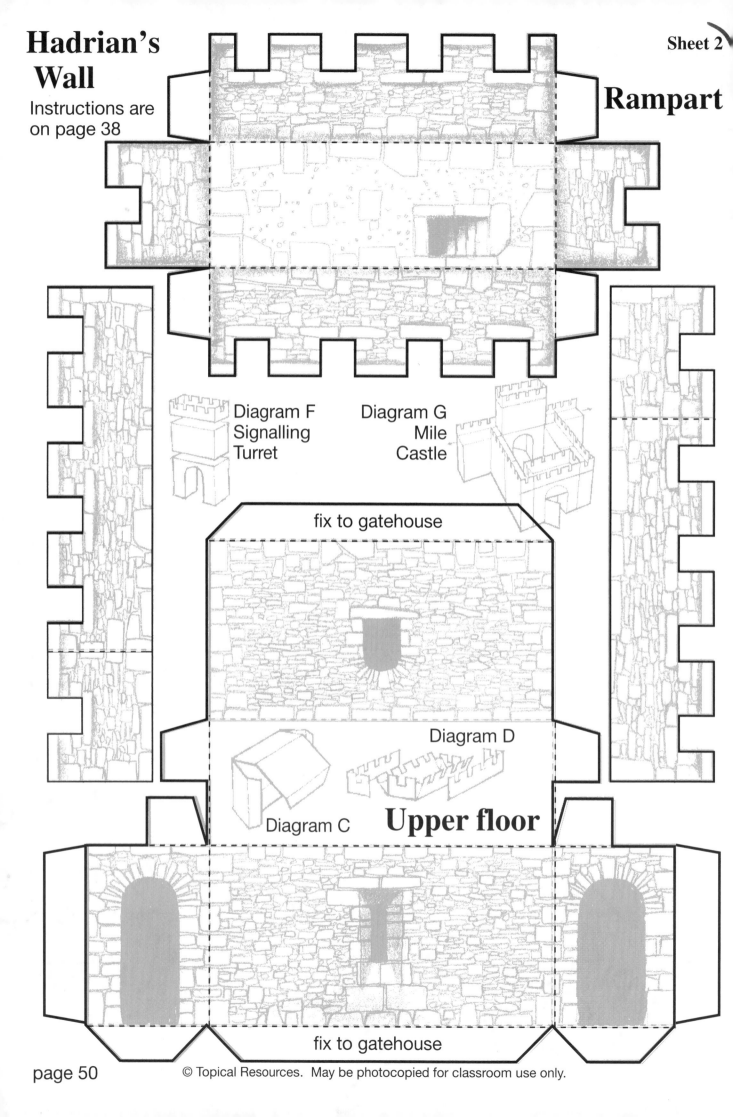

Hadrian's Wall

Instructions are on page 38

Rampart

Diagram F
Signalling
Turret

Diagram G
Mile
Castle

fix to gatehouse

Diagram D

Diagram C

Upper floor

fix to gatehouse

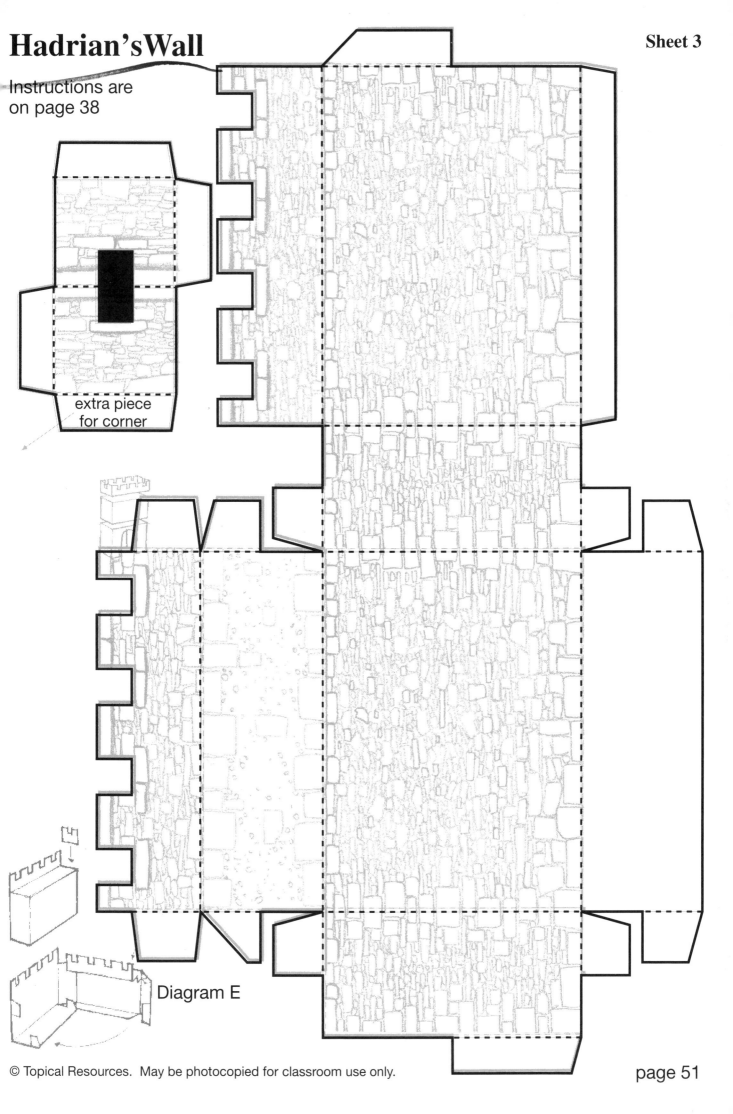

Hadrian's Wall

Instructions are
on page 38

extra piece
for corner

Diagram E

Everyday Life for Rich Roman Britons Living in Towns

Bedrooms
Rich families would have fine furniture and beds. They would use charcoal braziers to heat the rooms.

The Bathhouse and Lavatory
Rich Romans made a stream to run through the house to clear away the toilet waste and provide water for the baths.

The Dining Room
The room would have low couches by low tables for the family to eat their meals, served by slaves.

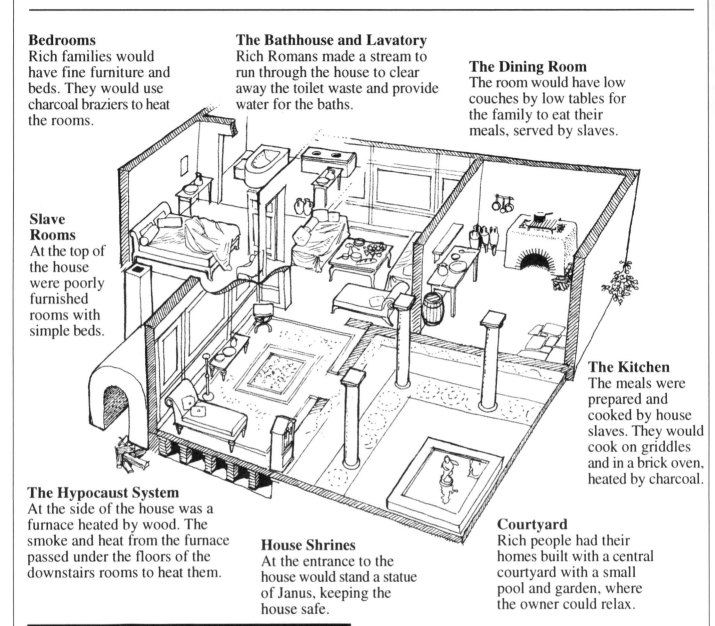

Slave Rooms
At the top of the house were poorly furnished rooms with simple beds.

The Kitchen
The meals were prepared and cooked by house slaves. They would cook on griddles and in a brick oven, heated by charcoal.

The Hypocaust System
At the side of the house was a furnace heated by wood. The smoke and heat from the furnace passed under the floors of the downstairs rooms to heat them.

House Shrines
At the entrance to the house would stand a statue of Janus, keeping the house safe.

Courtyard
Rich people had their homes built with a central courtyard with a small pool and garden, where the owner could relax.

Task - Finding Out About Aspects of the Period

Study the text and illustrations on pages 52 and 53 then complete your own copy of the chart below in as much detail as you can.

How do we know about rich Roman town houses?
Archaeologists have evacuated a house like this in Caerwent in Wales. They found that the Romans used stone, bricks and wood for building walls which were then covered with plaster. Tiles or slates were used for the roofing. Thick blue or green glass was used for the windows. Large quantities of small coloured tiles are evidence of extensive mosaics in the house.

Topic	A Rich Roman's House	A Poor Briton's House
Heating		
Cooking		
Washing		
Furniture		

Everyday Life for Poor Britons in Roman Britain

Beds
The poor Britons slept on piles of straw, and covered themselves with animal skins to keep warm.

Heating
A central wood fire would provide the only heat in the round stone or mud hut, which would have a very smoky atmosphere.

Cooking
An iron pot hanging over the fire would be the main way of cooking. A stone oven would be used to bake their bread.

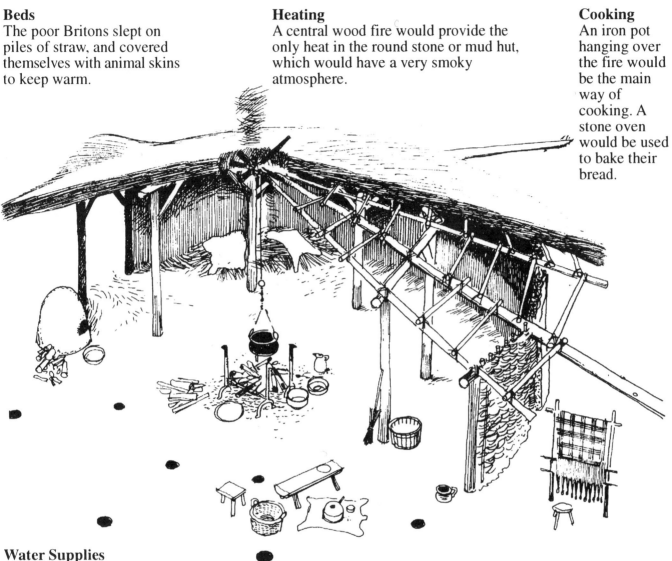

Water Supplies
Most poor Briton's homes were built close to a stream or spring of water. They rarely washed themselves.

Furniture
A few stools and a wooden table were the only pieces of furniture in the house.

Toilets
A poor Britain would have a pot by the wall to use as a toilet. When full it would be emptied into the midden outside.

Task - A Reasoning Exercise

1 After careful study of pages 52 and 53 choose which home you would have preferred to have lived in during Roman times in Britain. Give several reasons for your choice. Write your answers in full sentences.

2 Study pages 52 and 53 again. Now, list five things about the house that have changed from Roman Britain and five things that have stayed the same. Write your answers in full sentences.

Roman Writing and Mathematics

Task A - Make a Roman Writing Tablet

You will need three pieces of card cut out from a corrugated cardboard box, a ruler, pencils, scissors, glue, Plasticine, crayons or felt tip pens and a modelling tool.

3
Roll out a sheet of Plasticine about ½cm thick. cut it to the size of the 'window' shape in your frame.

Instructions

1

Draw three rectangles of the same size on a cardboard box. Cut them out carefully.

2

Draw frames with your ruler on two of the pieces of card. Now cut along these lines to make windows in two pieces of card.

4
Paste the two frames together on top of each other. Next paste these on top of the third rectangle of card. Fill in the window shape with Plasticine.

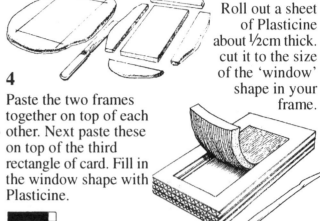

5

Decorate the frame with Roman scrolls. Use a modelling tool as a Roman stylus and write a message on your Roman writing tablet.

Roman Mathematics

The Romans wrote their numbers very differently from our own numbers. Here are the Roman numbers copied out for you:-

1 = I, 2 = II, 3 = III, 4 = IV, 5 = V, 6 = VI, 7 = VII, 8 = VIII, 9 = IX, 10 = X, 11 = XI, 12 = XII, 13 = XIII, 14 = XIV, 15 = XV, 16 = XVI, 17 = XVII, 18 = XVIII, 19 = XIX, 20 = XX, 30 = XXX, 40 = XL, 50 = L, 60 = LX, 70 = LXX, 80 = LXXX, 90 = XC, 100 = C, 200 = CC, 300 = CCC, 400 = CD, 500 = D, 600 = DC, 700 = DCC, 800 = DCCC, 900 = CM, 1000 = M, 1100 = MC, 1500 = MD, 1900 = MCM,

Task B - Roman Numerals

Write these modern numbers in Roman numerals:

Now, change these Roman numbers to modern numbers:

As an extra challenge, try setting out simple tens and units addition sums in Roman numerals and try to solve them.

31=	1998=	XLIII=	CCCX=
27=	2000=	XCVIII=	CCXC=
54=	1588=	LXIX=	MCMXVII=
76=	1815=	CCLXXIV=	
126=	1918=	MDCCCXV=	

Words the Romans Left Us

Chester

The Roman word for a military camp was **'castra'**. Over the centuries since the Romans ruled Britain this word has changed to become **'chester'**. Many places where the Romans built forts or camps soon had towns built around or near the fort. The places took the name of the camp. Many of these places still have the Roman word for camp at the end of the name. For example: **Manchester, Colchester, Winchester, Doncaster.**

Abbreviations

Many of the abbreviations used in modern books and writing come from the language the Romans spoke and wrote.

P.S. *post script* in Latin, meaning 'after the writing', something you add at the end of a letter.

NB. *nota bene* in latin meaning 'note well' or take special notice of.

e.g. *examlpi gratia* in latin, meaning 'for example'.

cf. *confera* in Latin, meaning 'compare with'

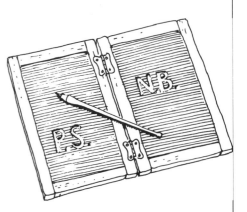

Prefixes and Suffixes

Many of our words have common beginnings and endings, which come from Latin words. Here are some examples:-

Ex- means 'out of' as in *exile*.

Pre- means 'before' as in *prepare*.

Sub- means 'beneath' as in *submarine*.

-ible means 'maybe' as in *possible*.

-able means 'must' as in *payable*.

-age means 'an action' as in *breakage*.

Months of the Year

January from the Roman God of the beginnings who faced both forwards and backwards.
February from the Roman word meaning to clean thoroughly.
March after the Roman God of Mars.
April from the Latin word meaning the opening of flowers.
May Maia was the Roman Goddess of warm weather.
June the month of the Goddess Juno who looked after women.

Task - Using Research Skills

1   Research in an atlas to find towns in Britain which have -*chester* or -*caster* at the end of their name; make a list of these names.

2   Use a dictionary to find five words with the prefix *pre*, five words starting in *ex* and five words with the prefix *sub* in them.

3   Two emperors gave their names to the months of July and August; research in reference books to find the emperor's names.

4   The last four months of our year are named after latin names for some numbers. Why were these numbers used?

The Story of Boudicca

Boudicca was the Queen of the Iceni, a tribe of Britons in AD 61.

She had long red hair and was a strong and fierce Queen.

Roman taxmen came to her tribe. They robbed the Queen.

Boudicca burnt Roman towns such as London, killing most of the people.

The Roman Army beat Boudicca. Most of her men were killed.

Boudicca killed herself rather than be captured by the Romans.

---

1   Boudicca was _____ of the Iceni, a tribe of _____ in A.D. 61.

2   She had long ____ hair and was a strong and _____ Queen.

3   Roman _____ came to her _____. They_____ the Queen.

4   Boudicca burnt _____ towns, such as _____, killing most of the people.

5   The _____ Army beat _____. Most of her men were killed.

6   Boudicca _____ herself, rather than be _____ by the Romans.

7   Carefully draw and colour your own picture of Boudicca on her chariot, charging into battle.

    Level 2

The Story of Boudicca

Boudicca became Queen of the Iceni tribe in East Anglia after her husband's death in A.D. 61. She was a strong and fierce lady with knee length red hair.

Some Roman taxmen visited her. They abused the Queen and her daughters and robbed them of their treasure. Boudicca decided to take her revenge against the Romans.

With help from her tribe, Boudicca attacked Roman towns including London, killing the people who lived there.

The Roman army beat Boudicca's tribesmen in a fierce battle. Eighty thousand of her people were killed. Rather than be captured by the Romans, Boudicca killed herself.

A

1 When did Boudicca become Queen of the Iceni Tribe?

2 Where did the Iceni Tribe live?

3 What did Boudicca look like?

4 How did the Roman taxmen treat Boudicca and her daughters?

5 Which Roman town did Boudicca attack?

6 Who beat Boudicca's army in battle?

B

1 Why do you think Boudicca wanted revenge against the Romans?

2 Why do you think that Boudicca did not want the Romans to capture

C

Carefully draw and colour your own picture of Boudicca on her war chariot charging into battle.

The Story of Boudicca

Anglesey

The final battle took place in the Midlands

Boudicca taking poison rather than be captured by the Romans

Boudicca was a Celtic princess who lived in East Anglia. She became Queen of her tribe in A.D. 61 when her husband died. Boudicca was a strong and fierce woman with knee length hair. Some Roman taxmen visited Boudicca's tribe, they abused Boudicca and her daughters and robbed her people.

Boudicca and her tribe wanted revenge against the Romans, so they attacked the nearby Roman town of Colchester, killing all the inhabitants. Next, Boudicca burnt and looted London, killing its people in horrible ways.

A Roman general, called Paulinus marched with his troops from Anglesey to fight the Celtic tribe lead by Boudicca. The battle took place in the Midlands of England. Boudicca led her men into battle riding in her chariot.

Eighty thousand of the Celts were killed in the fierce fight. Rather than be captured by the Romans, Boudicca poisoned herself.

A

1 When did Boudicca become Queen of the Iceni Tribe?

2 How did the Roman taxmen treat Boudicca and her people?

3 Why did Boudicca attack the Roman town of Colchester?

4 What did Boudicca do to the Roman city of London?

5 Who led the Roman army against the Celtic tribes?

6 What did Boudicca lead her army into battle in?

B

1 Why do you think Boudicca was described as fierce?

2 Why do you think Boudicca wanted revenge on the Romans?

3 Why do you think Paulinus led his army from North Wales?

4 Why do you think this battle took place in the Midlands?

5 Why didn't Boudicca want to be captured by the Romans?

C

Carefully draw and colour your own picture of Boudicca.

 Level 4

The Story of Boudicca

Boudicca was a fierce, strong and red-haired princess of the Iceni tribe, who became Queen on the death of her husband in A.D.61. Boudicca wanted to keep her tribe free of Roman ways. The Romans wanted to tax all the people of Britain to pay for their armies which were needed to keep the Celtic people under control. Roman taxmen visiting the Iceni treated Boudicca and her daughters very roughly. They abused and robbed the Queen, her family and tribe.

The Iceni were very angry and wished to have their revenge upon the occupying Romans. Led by the warrior Queen, they attacked the town of Camulodum, crying "Death to the Romans". The people of the town were killed. The wild Iceni moved on to Londinium, the Roman capital. Boudicca ordered it to be raised to the ground. The people of the city were killed in the Iceni tribe's rage. Fear spread throughout all the Roman settlements of Britain.

Hearing of these awful events in Anglesey, where he had been destroying the last stronghold of the Celtic Druid priests, Paulinus, the Roman general, marched his legions south to squash the tribes who had joined Boudicca in the Midlands of England. The well disciplined Roman army massacred the wild British tribes. Eighty thousand Celts died in the fierce battles.

Boudicca, who had led her warriors in their charge against the shield walls of the Roman army, fled from the terrible slaughter. She sought refuge in a nearby wood, where she poisoned herself and her daughters, rather than fall into the hands of the victorious Romans.

A

1   Why do you think Boudicca wanted to keep her people free from the influence of the Romans?

2   What action made the Iceni and Boudicca angry with the Romans?

3   Why do you think Boudicca attacked Camulodum?

4   What action spread fear throughout the settlements of Roman Britain?

5   Why do you think Paulinus was in Anglesey with his army?

6   Why do you think the Roman army defeated the Celts in the battle in the Midlands?

7   What is a massacre?

8   Why do you think that Boudicca was afraid of being captured by the Romans?

B

1   Define the words: disciplined and savage.

2   What evidence tells you that Boudicca was a fierce person?

3   What do you think made the Roman army disciplined?

4   Why do you think Boudicca fled into a wood at the end of the battle?

C

Use reference books to research

1   The Druid priests of the Celts.

2   Where the main towns of Roman Britain were situated.

Carefully illustrate your work.

The Romans Leave Britain

Forts were made along the south east coast to stop pirate raids from Germany 280 A.D.

Men from Scotland took over the Roman city of York in 367 A.D.

Many men were sent back to help save Rome in 398 A.D.

Wild tribes from Germany took over parts of the south of England 398 A.D..

Many people buried their riches to save them from robbers from over the sea.

Rome was being attacked. It could not help Britain any longer.

1   Forts were made along the _____ ____ coast to stop _____ raids.

2   Men from _____ took over the Roman city of ____ in 367 A.D.

3   Many men were sent back to help save _____ in 398 A.D.

4   Wild _____ from _____ took over parts of the _____ of England 398 A.D.

5   Many people _____their _____ to save them from robbers from over the ___.

6   Rome was being _____. It could not ____ Britain any longer.

7   Carefully draw your own picture of the pirates attacking Roman Britain.

 Level 2

The Romans Leave Britain

The Romans were attacked by pirates from Germany in A.D. 280. The Romans made forts along the south-east coast of England to stop these raiders.

The Picts and Scots from Scotland captured the city of York chasing out all the Romans in A.D. 367

As Rome was being robbed from the east, many Roman soldiers from Britain were sent to help. Tribes from Germany were robbing towns in the south of England in A.D. 398

Many people started to bury their riches to hide them from robbers from overseas. As Rome was attacked by wild tribes from the east it could no longer send help to Britain. This was the end of Roman control of Britain.

A

1 When was Roman Britain first attacked by pirates from Germany?

2 Where did the Picts come from to capture the city of York in A.D. 367?

3 What did the tribes from Germany do in A.D. 398 ?

4 Why did people start to bury their riches?

5 Why could Rome not send help to Britain in A.D. 410?

B

1 Why do yo think the tribes from Germany kept robbing Britain?

2 Why did Britain build forts in A.D. 280?

C

Carefully draw and colour your own picture of pirates attacking Roman Britain.

The Romans Leave Britain

From about A.D. 250 tribes from Germany and southern Europe raided the edges of the Roman Empire. The Romans called these raiders 'Barbarians'. The Roman rulers would call Roman soldiers back from Britain to help fight against these attackers.

In A.D. 368 Picts and Scots tribesmen from north of Hadrian's wall attacked York. The Roman soldiers defending the city, fled south. The Picts and Scots returned home with many treasures they had taken from the rich merchants of York.

Many Saxon sea pirates from Germany, raided Roman Britain towns and villas from A.D. 280. The Romans built forts along the coast to try to stop these raids. People in Roman Britain often buried their treasure to keep it safe from these raiders. Many of these buried treasure hordes have been found since.

When Italy and Rome, at the heart of the Roman Empire, were attacked in A.D. 410 the Emperor Honorious ordered all Roman soldiers back to Rome to help fight the barbarian attackers. He told the people of Britain they would have to defend themselves against Saxon raiders. This was the end of Roman control of Britain.

A

1   Why did the Romans build forts along the south-east coast of England after A.D. 280?

2   Where did the people of Britain put their treasure when they heard of the attacks of the Saxon pirates?

3   Why did the Roman rulers call troops back from Britain after A.D. 280?

4   Where did the Picts and Scots attack in A.D. 367?

5   How did the Roman soldiers of York react to the Scots and Picts in A.D. 367?

6   Why did Emperor Honorious order soldiers back to Rome in A.D. 410?

7   What did Emperor Honorious tell the people of Britain in A.D. 410?

B

1   What evidence suggests that the people of Britain were afraid of Saxon pirates?

2   Why do you think Saxon pirates came to Britain?

3   Why do you think the Barbarians attacked Rome?

4   Why do you think the people of Britain were worried in A.D. 410?

5   What evidence tells you that Emperor Honorious was short of soldiers in Rome in A.D. 410?

C

Carefully draw and colour your own picture of Saxon pirates attacking Roman Britain.

       Level 4

The Romans Leave Britain

From A.D. 280, Roman Britain was raided by Saxon pirates from Germany. In an effort to stop the raids, a line of forts was built along the south coast by the Romans. However, these raids continued to threaten the towns of Roman Britain.

Raiding Picts and Scots' tribesmen from north of Hadrian's wall reached as far south as York in 367 A.D. The Roman legion defending the city was chased away, and the rich merchants homes were looted by the wild robbers, who carried their loot back over the wall.

Many tribes from Germany, France and southern Europe raided the frontier towns of the Roman Empire. These tribes were called 'Barbarians', because of their wild and barbaric behaviour. At first these tribes only raided the edge of the Roman world, but soon, because of the weak Roman Emperors, or quarrelling generals, Barbarians were attacking Roman cities at the heart of the Roman empire.

The rulers in Rome would often send for legions in Britain to return to help fight off the raids from the barbarian Visigoths, Vandals and Goth tribes. This left many areas of Britain without the protection of the Roman army.

As Saxon raids became more frequent, the people of Roman Britain often buried their treasure when raiders threatened from over the seas. Many of these treasure hordes have been found in different parts of Britain. In A.D. 410 The Roman Emperor Honorious wrote to the British cities, telling them that they would have to defend themselves as all the Roman soldiers were needed to defend Italy and Rome itself. This marked the end of Roman control of Britain.

A

1   Why do you think the Romans built forts along the south coast of Britain in A.D. 280?

2   What do you think the Saxon pirates were coming to Britain for?

3   Why do you think the Picts and Scots picked rich merchants' homes to loot in York in A.D. 367?

4   What did the Picts and Scots carry back to their homes in A.D. 367?

5   Why do you think the Romans called the raiders from Germany, France and southern Europe, 'Barbarians'?

6   Why do you think that the raiders from outside the Roman empire were soon able to attack the heart of the Empire?

7   Why do you think Roman Britons might want to bury their riches after A.D. 367?

8   Why do you think the Emperor Honorius told Roman Britain's cities they would have to defend themselves?

B

1   Define the words:
    Pirate, Emperor and Vandals

2   Why do you think many Roman treasure hordes have been found in Britain?

3   What do you understand by 'barbaric' behavior?

4   What caused the end of Roman rule in Britain?

C

Use reference books to research
    (i) The weapons and armour of Saxon raiders of Roman Britain.
    (ii) The tribes called Visigoths, Vandals and Goths.   *Carefully illustrate your work.*

Time to Spare Activities

1 Write a House Slave's diary for a day in Roman Londinium.

2 Write a letter from Julius Caesar to his wife in Rome telling her what Britain is like.

3 Make a model of one of the Roman Gods.

4 Make a Roman Bedroom in a shoebox.

5 Design and make a Chariot like Boudicca's warriors used.

6 Draw a picture of shops in a Roman Britain town.

7 Research all you can about the ships that the Saxon pirates sailed in.

8 Write the diary of a Roman shopkeeper in Londinium for three days.

9 Design your own legion's badge and standard.

10 Find out how the Romans gave Britain its name.

11 Draw the weapons a Roman Gladiator might use.

12 Produce some addition sums using Roman numerals.

13 Research as much as you can about the Emperor Hadrian.

14 Design your own shrine for a Roman God.

15 Make a poster of Roman land transport.

16 Research the history of a local Roman fort.

17 List the equipment in a modern kitchen and compare it with a Roman Kitchen.

18 Write a diary as if you were a Celt witnessing the Roman invasion of Britain.

19 Make a poster advertising a Gladiator show in a Roman British town.

20 Make your own booklet of the designs of pottery in Roman Britain.

21 Research as much as you can about the games children played in Roman Britain.

22 Design your own Celtic Briton's shield.

23 Make a model of a Roman ballista.

24 Choose a year in Roman Britain times and find out as much as you can about that year.

25 Make your own booklet about the Roman Army

26 Make your own Mosaic to commemorate some special event in your family's life.

27 Make a poster illustrating Roman British coins.

28 Make your own catalogue of Roman and Celtic jewellery.

29 Make your own map of the roads the Romans built in Britain.

30 Make a mask for an actor in a Roman Theatre.

31 Research all you can about the Roman General Agricola.

32 Make your own poster display of fashions in dress in Roman Britain.